Editor
Eric Migliaccio

Editorial Project Manager
Ina Massler Levin, M.A.

Editor in Chief
Sharon Coan, M.S. Ed.

Illustrator
Howard Chaney

Cover Artist
Denise Bauer

Art Coordinator
Denice Adorno

Creative Director
Elayne Roberts

Imaging
Alfred Lau
James Edward Grace

Product Manager
Phil Garcia

Publishers
Rachelle Cracchiolo, M.S. Ed.
Mary Dupuy Smith, M.S. Ed.

Challenging

Author

Tom Burt

Teacher Created Materials, Inc.
6421 Industry Way
Westminster, CA 92683
www.teachercreated.com
ISBN-1-57690-391-5
©2000 Teacher Created Materials, Inc.
Made in U.S.A.

Table of Contents

Table of Contents

Basketball

Hockey

Other Sports and Activities

Scavenger Hunt Answer Sheet

Introduction

Sports Page Scavenger Hunts & Other Activities is intended for middle elementary grades through middle school, but the activities may be applicable for younger students interested in sports. These activities will require the teacher to have access to a sports page each day, especially during football, basketball, and baseball seasons. The workbook is divided into sections according to individual sports or events. Refer to the table of contents for a listing of individual activities.

Most of the activities may be used with an entire class, but many of the activities may be used with individuals or small groups. In addition, the teacher may want to divide the class into groups and have friendly competitions. (Many of the games and activities in this workbook are competitive by nature. Be sure to talk to students about using good sportsmanship during class activities. Inform students that displays of poor sportsmanship may result in non-participation for upcoming activities.) Teachers may use the activities to motivate students to turn in missing assignments or as a behavior modification. Because of the high interest level that sports generate, students will work hard in other curricular areas in order to participate in sporting activities. You may also wish to incorporate activities from this workbook into your daily curriculum. Many activities involve math concepts such as decimals, fractions, or percentages. Students will find sports-related themes a good basis for research or independent study. Many activities from this workbook are suitable for extra-credit assignments as well. Student interest will dictate the use of each activity. For example, a basketball activity may generate interest for the entire class. A golf activity may be of interest to only certain individuals.

The scavenger hunts are at the beginning of each section. Students will work in groups or individually to find the list of items as quickly as possible. Participants will cut and paste their answers in the appropriate numbered box on the worksheet titled "Scavenger Hunt Answer Sheet" (page 144). The teacher will need to act as the judge for these activities because most answers will be subjective. The Scavenger Hunts are numbered from easiest to most difficult. For instance, "Basketball Scavenger Hunt #1" is the easiest in that section, while "Basketball Scavenger Hunt #10" is the most difficult. The football scavenger hunts will work best with a sports page from Monday during the football season because students will need to refer to box scores for answers. The other sports are played during the week, and box scores are usually listed on a daily basis. Box scores, which tell individual statistics for a sporting event, are always printed the day after the event. Many activities in this workbook rely on box scores. For reference, sample box scores for each of the four major team sports in the United States and Canada have been provided. These box scores can be found on pages 9 (baseball), 39 (football), 71 (basketball), and 94 (hockey).

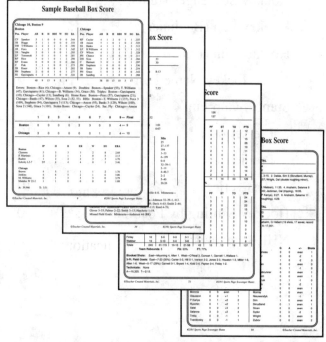

(The box scores shown on these pages were created and are not exact replicas of box scores from actual games. The players, however, are real. In some cases, the players were chosen from throughout the history of the sport, and in other cases, they were chosen from a team's actual roster—or an All-Star roster—during a given year.)

Introduction *(cont.)*

Some games and activities in this workbook will require students to choose players or teams in a specific order. Use the workbook page titled "The Draft" on page 143 to help in this process. Make a copy of the page and cut the numbered rectangles on the lines. You may want to laminate the rectangles for durability before use. Put the numbers in a hat or other container and allow students to draw out numbers to determine order. The activities approximate the way that actual professional sports teams assemble their rosters. During its offseason, each sport holds a draft during which players from the college (and in some sports, high school) ranks are selected (i.e., drafted) based on their perceived potential. The draft order is generally determined by each team's performance during the most recently completed season (i.e., the team with the worst record drafts first in the following draft, the team that won the championship drafts last, etc.).

Timing is important when using *Sports Page Scavenger Hunts.* The teacher will need to become involved, keeping track of the schedules of teams. For example, most of the football activities will have to be completed on Friday before students leave for the weekend because most of the games take place on Saturday and Sunday. Basketball and baseball activities can take place throughout the week and on weekends because games are scheduled daily. Daily sports pages always have schedules of upcoming games. Allow student helpers to review the sports page for upcoming schedules and events. Many students will volunteer to read the sports page on a daily basis. This will save the teacher time and familiarize students with the sports page.

Sometimes games are played on non-traditional days. For instance, football games are played on Thursday nights occasionally. Most other professional and college football games are played on weekends. Baseball, basketball, and hockey games may be played on any night of the week. Adjust activities for students accordingly. (For a breakdown on the months of the year during which certain sports are played, please see page 7.)

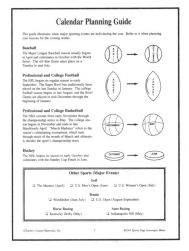

Before using the activities in this workbook, the teacher should familiarize him- or herself with the organization of the sports page. Statistics and schedules are usually printed on the same day each week. For example, baseball statistics may come out each Wednesday. The teacher will need to post the statistics that day for certain activities.

Some of the activities in this workbook will run through the duration of a sporting season. You may wish to copy and organize pages into booklets or binders for students to keep in their desks so they are less likely to lose them.

Start a collection of newspapers in the classroom. Have students bring papers from home. Set aside a table or counter and organize them into sections. This way the sports page will be handy for activities in this workbook.

In addition, most newspaper publications will give free or reduced subscriptions to schools. Inquire at a nearby daily newspaper to see if the publication will help you to obtain a copy of the newspaper for your classroom each day.

Commonly Used Abbreviations

Baseball

AB	At Bat(s)
H	Hit(s)
R	Run(s)
HR	Home Run(s)
SB	Stolen Bases
RBI	Run(s) Batted In
BB	Base on Balls (also, W = Walks)
SO	Strike Out(s)
IP	Innings Pitched
HBP	Hit by Pitch
DP	Double Play
BA	Batting Average
ERA	Earned Run Average
ER	Earned Run(s)
MLB	Major League Baseball
AL	American League
NL	National League
P	Pitcher
C	Catcher
1B	First Base
2B	Second Base
3B	Third Base
SS	Shortstop
LF	Left Field
CF	Center field
RF	Right Field
E	Error

Football

NFL	National Football League
NFC	National Football Conference
AFC	American Football Conference
NCAA	National College Athletic Association
TD	Touchdown(s)
REC	Reception(s)
PAT	Point After Touchdown(s)
ATT	Rushing/Passing Attempt(s)
FG	Field Goal(s)
YDS	Yards
INT	Interception(s)

Offensive Positions:

QB	Quarterback
RB	Running Back
HB	Halfback
FB	Fullback
WR	Wide Receiver
TE	Tight End
OL	Offensive Lineman
K	Kicker

Defensive Postitions:

DL	Defensive Lineman
LB	Linebacker
CB	Cornerback
FS	Free Safety
SS	Strong Safety
P	Punter

Basketball

G	Guard
F	Forward
C	Center
NBA	National Basketball Association
FG	Field Goal(s)
FT	Free Throw(s)
A	Assist(s)
REB	Rebound(s)
BLK	Blocked Shots(s)
PF	Personal Foul(s)

Other Sports and General Terms

NHL	National Hockey League
MLS	Major League Soccer
G	Goal
PF	Points For
PA	Points Against
(L)PGA	(Ladies) Professional Golfer's Association
W	Wins
L	Losses
T	Ties
PCT	Percentage
GB	Games Back (in standings)
MVP	Most Valuable Player

Calendar Planning Guide

This guide illustrates when major sporting events are held during the year. Refer to it when planning your lessons for the coming weeks.

Baseball

The Major League Baseball season usually begins in April and culminates in October with the World Series. The All-Star Game takes place on a Tuesday in mid-July.

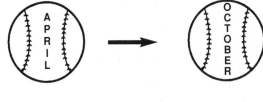

Professional and College Football

The NFL begins its regular season in early September. The Super Bowl has traditionally been played on the last Sunday in January. The college football season begins in late August, and the Bowl Games are played in mid-December through the beginning of January.

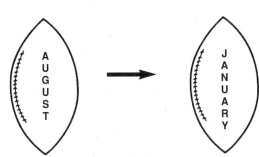

Professional and College Basketball

The NBA extends from early November through the championship series in June. The college season begins in November and ends in late March/early April. "March Madness" refers to the season's culminating tournament, which lasts through much of the month of March and ultimately decides the sport's championship team.

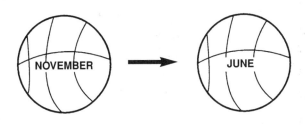

Hockey

The NHL begins its season in early October and culminates with the Stanley Cup Finals in June.

Other Sports (Major Events)

Golf

❏ The Masters (April)   ❏ U.S. Men's Open (June)   ❏ U.S. Women's Open (July)

Tennis

❏ Wimbledon (June–July)   ❏ U.S. Open (August–September)

Horse Racing

❏ Kentucky Derby (May)

Auto Racing

❏ Indianapolis 500 (May)

First Day Sports Scramble

Fill out this worksheet at the beginning of the school year. Answers should be based on the last completed season/event prior to the first day of school. You will receive a number of points (in parentheses) for each correct response. Total the points after all the events have been completed and see if your sports knowledge is greater than that of your classmates!

Student Name _____

Women's US Open Tennis Champion _____ (10)

Men's US Open Tennis Champion _____ (10)

American League Baseball Champion _____ (5)

National League Baseball Champion _____ (5)

World Series Champion _____ (10)

NCAA Football Champion _____ (10)

American Football Conference Champion _____ (5)

National Football Conference Champion _____ (5)

Super Bowl Champion _____ (10)

NCAA Men's Basketball Final Four Contestants

_____ (5) _____ (5) _____ (5) _____ (5)

NCAA Men's Basketball Champion _____ (10)

NCAA Women's Basketball Final Four Contestants

_____ (5) _____ (5) _____ (5) _____ (5)

NCAA Women's Basketball Champion _____ (10)

Masters Golf Champion _____ (10)

Stanley Cup Hockey Champion _____ (10)

Indianapolis 500 Winner _____ (10)

Total your points and write the result here. _____

Sample Baseball Box Score

Chicago 10, Boston 9

Boston

Pos.	Player	AB	R	H	RBI	W	SO	BA
CF	Speaker	5	1	1	0	0	0	.344
3B	Boggs	5	1	1	0	0	0	.333
DH	T.Williams	2	2	2	2	3	0	.399
1B	Foxx	3	1	2	3	0	1	.345
1B	Vaughn	2	0	1	0	0	1	.293
LF	Ystrzmski	3	0	1	0	1	0	.301
RF	Rice	3	0	1	0	1	2	.298
RF	Evans	0	0	0	0	0	0	.266
C	Fisk	3	1	1	0	0	1	.273
2B	Doerr	3	1	0	0	1	2	.282
PH	Stephens	2	0	0	1	0	1	.277
SS	Garciaparra	4	2	4	3	0	0	.324
		40	**9**	**14**	**9**	**5**	**8**	

Chicago

Pos.	Player	AB	R	H	RBI	W	SO	BA
RF	Cuyler	4	1	2	0	1	1	.337
1B	Anson	5	1	0	1	0	2	.325
SS	Banks	4	1	1	3	1	2	.313
LF	B.Williams	4	1	2	0	1	1	.312
CF	Wilson	4	1	2	1	1	2	.328
PH	Chance	0	1	0	0	0	0	.311
DH	Sosa	5	3	2	2	0	2	.266
C	Hartnett	3	0	1	0	1	1	.297
PH	Stephnsn	1	0	0	0	0	1	.336
3B	Santo	3	0	0	0	0	3	.254
PH	Grace	1	0	1	3	0	0	.342
2B	Sandbrg	4	1	2	0	0	2	.288
		38	**10**	**13**	**10**	**5**	**17**	

Errors: Boston—Rice (4); Chicago—Anson (9). Doubles: Boston—Speaker (53), T. Williams (47), Garciaparra (41); Chicago—B. Williams (34), Grace (50). Triples: Boston—Garciaparra (10); Chicago—Cuyler (13), Sandberg (6). Home Runs: Boston—Foxx (57), Garciaparra (21); Chicago—Banks (47), Wilson (35), Sosa 2 (52, 53). RBI: Boston—T. Williams 2 (137), Foxx 3 (169), Stephens (94), Garciaparra 3 (113); Chicago—Anson (93), Banks 3 (129), Wilson (100), Sosa 2 (146), Grace 3 (101). Stolen Bases: Chicago—Cuyler (24). Sac. Fly: Chicago—Anson

	1	2	3	4	5	6	7	8	9 — Final
Boston	0	0	0	0	2	3	0	0	4 — 9
Chicago	3	0	0	0	0	0	1	2	4 — 10

	IP	H	R	ER	W	SO	ERA
Boston							
Clemens	5	5	3	3	2	8	2.68
P. Martinez	2	2	1	1	0	5	2.13
Radetz	1	2	2	2	3	3	2.76
Eckrsly L 3–7	2/3	4	4	4	0	1	3.46
Chicago							
Brown	4	5	1	1	1	2	1.76
Jenkins	4	7	5	2	1	6	3.06
M. Williams	0	1	3	3	3	0	3.79
Maddux W 22–2	1	1	0	0	0	0	1.88

A: 39,966   **T:** 3:31

Baseball Scavenger Hunt #1

Find the following from the sports page and glue them on your Scavenger Hunt Answer Sheet.

1. the word *baseball*

2. a picture of a baseball player

3. the name of any baseball team

4. a player who hit a ball

5. a team that is named for a bird

6. the word *outfield*

7. a score from a game

8. a team that scored more than four runs

9. the name of a pitcher

10. a team that has one syllable in its team name

Baseball Scavenger Hunt #2

Find the following from the sports page and glue them on your Scavenger Hunt Answer Sheet.

1. the name of a player whose last name ends in **n**

2. the word *runs*

3. a player who hit a home run

4. a picture of a baseball bat

5. a team that scored one run in the first inning

6. a quote from a baseball player

7. a player who plays shortstop

8. a team that won by at least three runs

9. a game that lasted over three hours

10. a team that is not named for an animal

Baseball Scavenger Hunt #3

Find the following from the sports page and glue them on your answer sheet.

1. a team name that is a person

2. the word *National*

3. a picture of a baseball or softball

4. a player who had at least two hits in a game

5. a game that was attended by more than 16,000 fans

6. a game that was played outdoors

7. a player whose last name begins with **M**

8. the name of a baseball field or stadium

9. a person who writes about baseball games

10. the time that a baseball game starts

Baseball Scavenger Hunt #4

Find the following from the sports page and glue them on your answer sheet.

1. a player who pitched fewer than three innings

2. a team that lost by more than four runs

3. a game that was played at night

4. a picture of a person throwing or catching a ball

5. the word *innings*

6. the name of a catcher

7. a team that scored an even number of runs

8. a logo of any baseball team

9. the name of any baseball team within 100 miles of your school

10. a player who has less than four syllables in his first and last names

Baseball Scavenger Hunt #5

Find the following from the sports page and glue them on your answer sheet.

1. a headline that has the name of a professional baseball team

2. a picture of a baseball player wearing a white jersey

3. the word *swing*

4. a team that has an infielder as its leadoff hitter

5. a city that hosted a major league baseball game

6. a team that scored a number of runs that is a multiple of three

7. a visiting team that won

8. a baseball player whose first or last name ends in a vowel

9. a game score that totaled more than 10 runs

10. a proper noun from a baseball article

Baseball Scavenger Hunt #6

Find the following from the sports page and glue them on your answer sheet.

1. a game that went into extra innings

2. a player who bats fourth in the lineup

3. a pitcher who gave up more than three hits

4. a picture of any baseball player wearing a batting helmet

5. a team that hit more than one home run

6. the letters **AB** from a box score

7. a team that scored runs in the eighth inning

8. a player who made an error

9. a team that has a winning record

10. a fraction or decimal from a box score or baseball article

Baseball Scavenger Hunt #7

Find the following from the sports page and glue them on your answer sheet.

1. a team that played in another country

2. a player who had two RBI

3. the word *plate*

4. an adjective from a baseball headline

5. any baseball game where no team scored in the first two innings

6. a team that scored runs close to the numeric value of *pi*

7. a pitcher who had more than five strikeouts

8. an attendance figure where the sum of the digits is greater than 20

9. a picture of a manager or umpire

10. the name of a female baseball (or softball) player

Baseball Scavenger Hunt #8

Find the following from the sports page and glue them on your answer sheet.

1. the word *umpire*

2. any town or city that hosted a baseball game and begins with **N**

3. a pitcher who won a game

4. an adverb from a baseball article

5. score of the losing team divided by the score of the winning team is 0.5

6. a picture of a ball or bat in an advertisement

7. an attendance figure that is divisible by three

8. a team that has lost at least 10 more games than it has won

9. an apostrophe from a baseball article

10. a player who had three hits in one game

Baseball Scavenger Hunt #9

Find the following from the sports page and glue them on your answer sheet.

1. a picture of a mitt

2. a game that was played indoors

3. the letters **IP**

4. a pitcher who gave up more than five hits

5. a total score that ended in a square number

6. a preposition from an article about baseball

7. the word *infield*

8. a team that has won five or more games than it has lost

9. a player who has the long /**o**/ sound in his name

10. a game that was attended by a number with a two in the ones place

Baseball Scavenger Hunt #10

Find the following from the sports page and glue them on your answer sheet.

1. a picture of a batting glove

2. an odd number on a player's jersey

3. a Little League team or an adult league team in your area

4. a pitcher who had more walks than strikeouts

5. a batter who hit 50% for one game

6. a game that ended after 8.5 innings

7. a verb from a headline for a baseball article

8. the word *double*

9. the name of a third baseman

10. a player who got a hit exactly one-third of his times at bat

Baseball Fun

Beginner

Students will choose baseball players from the box score section of the sports page to make an imaginary team of their own. Make sure students are able to locate players by position before you begin this activity. In the box scores, find the team statistics and explain to students the abbreviations used for each player position. (If you are unfamiliar with these, use the page in this workbook titled "Commonly Used Abbreviations" on page 6.) Make copies of the worksheet "Baseball Fun (Beginner)" on page 16 and give one to each participating student. This activity will work equally well with two or more players.

Have students search the box-score section of the sports page to find their teams. Make sure that students choose players from different teams. For example, if a student chooses a third baseman from the Boston Red Sox, that is the only player he or she may choose from the Red Sox in completing the roster. Also, make sure that this activity is held when there is a full slate of major league games. (During the major league season, many teams have Mondays and/or Thursdays off.) Otherwise, students will have to wait too long for results.

My Team	
2B	Jackie Robinson
LF	Stan Musial
CF	Willie Mays
1B	Lou Gehrig
C	Mike Piazza
3B	George Brett
RF	Roberto Clemente
SS	Alex Rodriguez
P	Sandy Koufax

After students complete their rosters, they will wait until the next day to see how their players fared. Allow students to go to the sports page to see how many runs their players scored. Have students list the required information on the worksheet next to the player's name. Students must record the information from the player's next game; otherwise, they will wait until their player has a good game, and the activity would go on too long. If students record information from the box score of the next game, the activity should last no longer than two or three days.

Students will record the runs and the runs batted in for their players as their total score. Also, keep track of home runs. You may wish to offer a special prize for the student whose team has the most home runs. Total the scores. See which student has the most runs and runs batted in. The winner will have the highest total.

If you are working on a particular math lesson, you may wish to use this activity as an extension. For example, what percentage of your team's runs did the catcher score? Students could practice changing a fraction to a decimal, and then to a percent. You may also wish to use "Computing Batting Averages" on pages 27 and 28 as a related activity.

As a variation, allow students to look up games and statistics on the Internet. Most professional teams have a Web site that can be easily accessed. Also, many newspapers are published online, and students can learn how to log on to their favorite sports page.

Baseball Fun

Beginner *(cont.)*

Position	Player	Runs (R)	Batted In (RBI)	Home Runs (HR)
Catcher				
Shortstop				
First Base				
Second Base				
Third Base				
Right Field				
Left Field				
Center Field				

Total number of runs scored by your team _____

Total number of runs batted in by your team _____

Add the number of runs and the number of runs batted in _____

This is your point total. Compare to other members of the class to see how you did!

Baseball Fun

Expert

In this activity, students will build their own team and compete against an imaginary pitching staff from the sports page. You will need to give each student copies of the two worksheets: "Baseball Fun: Batter (Expert)" on page 18 and "Baseball Fun: Pitcher (Expert)" on page 19. You may present this activity to one student or an entire class. This activity should be presented when you are working in curricular areas that are relevant to computing baseball statistics. You may consider presenting the activity when you are working on one or more of the following areas: fractions, long division, percentages, or decimals.

Have students go to the sports page to find their imaginary teams. Students will find a player for each of the positions at the top of the batter worksheet. The activity will work best if you allow students to take only one player from each team. For example, if a shortstop is taken from the Atlanta Braves, the student should not take another player from the Braves. Fill in the top part of the worksheet by choosing players from different teams until the roster is complete. Allow students to choose a designated hitter as well. This player may bat from any position, including the ones already chosen, as long as he comes from a different team. Then have students decide which team they will use as their pitching staff and write the team in the space provided. The remainder of the information on the pitcher worksheet will not be filled out until the team plays their next game because we do not know who the pitchers will be and how many the team will use in a game.

It may take more than one day to complete the remainder of the worksheets. Have the sports page in the classroom each day after you assign the activity. Most baseball teams play five to six days a week during the season, so students should not have to wait more than a day or two to complete their worksheets. Make sure that students use the very next game for each player on the roster. Do not allow students to bypass a player's game because of a bad performance. Have students fill in the required information on their worksheets.

To find the score of the game, record the number of runs that the players made and total it in the space provided. Then look at the statistics for the pitchers. Find the total number of runs that the pitchers gave up. The student must score more runs than his pitching staff gave up to win the contest. If the pitching team gave up more runs than the batting team scored, then the student loses the game. Write the final scores in the blanks provided at the bottom of the worksheet. Remember that all the blanks on the pitching staff may not be filled, depending on how many pitchers the team used for a game.

Have students compare their teams to see which team scored the highest. Find out how many students were able to win their games. Examine the worksheets to see if students chose many of the same players. Find out which player at each position was picked the most. This information could be used to create a class graph.

Baseball Fun: Batter

Expert *(cont.)*

Choose players, using the box scores. Then fill in their statistics after the next game they play.

Position	Player	AB	R	H	RBI
First Base					
Second Base					
Third Base					
Shortstop					
Catcher					
Right Field					
Left Field					
Center Field					
Designated Hitter					

	AB	R	H	RBI
Totals				

Total number of runs scored _____

Baseball Fun: Pitcher

Expert *(cont.)*

Name the team you wish to use as your pitching staff. _____

Use the statistics from the next game that they pitch to fill in the chart below.

Pitcher's Name	IP	H	R	ER	BB	SO

	IP	H	R	ER	BB	SO
Totals						

Write the number of runs your team scored from the batter worksheet. _____

Write the number of runs your pitching staff gave up. _____

If your team scored more runs than the pitching staff gave up, you win the game!

Major League Baseball Name Fun

Find on the sports page professional baseball teams that fit the descriptions below. Cut out the names and glue them in the spaces provided.

1. You go out on a boat to catch this team. _____

2. This team has deadly fangs. _____

3. This team might arrest you. _____

4. This team's members wear brown robes. _____

5. This team is hard to hit. _____

6. You can throw this team in the dryer. _____

7. This team is made up of baby bears. _____

8. This team will jump on your ship. _____

9. Scarlet, crimson, and maroon belong on this team. _____

10. This team might put feathers in their hats. _____

11. This team looks like itself. _____

12. This team is happy at sea. _____

13. This team's members have halos over their heads. _____

Teacher Note: Fold answers under before photocopying this page for students.

Answers

1. Marlins 2. Diamondbacks 3. Rangers 4. Padres 5. Dodgers 6. Red Sox, White Sox 7. Cubs
8. Pirates 9. Reds 10. Yankees 11. Twins 12. Mariners, Pirates 13. Angels

World Series Fun

Pre-series

Look at the sports page the week before the World Series. Find answers to the following questions.

1. Which team won more games during the regular season? _____

2. Which team gave up the most runs during the playoffs? _____

3. Does each team have a pitcher who won at least 15 games during the regular season? If so, name those pitchers. _____

   _____

4. Which team has the highest team batting average? _____

5. Name the batters from each team with the highest averages. _____

   _____

6. Which team had the most steals during the regular season? _____

7. Which player from either team had the most steals? _____

8. Which pitcher from either team had the lowest ERA? _____

9. Name the HR leaders from both teams and the number of home runs that they hit during the regular season. _____

10. Of the two teams in the Wolrd Series, which one's stadium has the larger capacity. _____

11. How many people do both stadiums combined hold? _____

12. Name the starting pitchers for Game 1. _____

13. Which city will host Game 1? _____

14. Will any of the games be played on artificial turf? _____

15. Name the pitcher from either team that had the most strikeouts during the regular season. _____ How many strikeouts did he have? _____

World Series Fun *(cont.)*

Predictions

Complete this activity before the World Series begins. Have this sheet with you as you watch the Series. Do not change any of your answers after the games begin. Point values are in parentheses after each question. Count the number of points you get throughout the series and write the total on the bottom.

1. Who will be the first to cross home plate in the Series? _____(5)

2. Name the player to be walked first in the Series. _____(5)

3. Name the first player to get a base hit in the Series. _____(5)

4. Do you think at least one game will go to extra innings? _____(3)

5. Name the total number of runs scored in Game four. _____(5)

6. How many pitchers will the visiting team use in Game 3? _____(3)

7. How many games will the series last? _____(3)

8. How many hits will the home team have in Game 2? _____(5)

9. How many home runs will be hit in the Series? _____(5)

10. How many batters will be walked in Game 1? _____(5)

11. Who will be the first player to steal a base in the Series? _____(5)

12. Which team will win the World Series? _____(7)

Total points and write here _____

World Series Fun (cont.)

Post-series

Use the sports page from the day after the World Series ends to find answers to the following.

1. Who was the MVP for the Series?_____

2. Who had the highest batting average for the Series? _____

3. How many fans attended the last game? _____

4. Which pitcher won the final game of the Series? _____

5. Who hit the most home runs for the Series?_____

6. Which team had the most hits for the Series?_____

7. How many games did the Series last? _____

8. What was the total number of runs scored by both teams in the Series?

9. Which pitcher had the most strikeouts in the Series? _____

10. How many games went to extra innings? _____

11. Name the player from each team who led his team in total hits, and tell how many hits each player had. _____

    _____

12. Which player scored the most runs in the Series? _____

13. Who were the RBI leaders for each team in the Series, and how many RBI did each player have? _____

14. Which team led the Series in errors committed?_____

15. How many errors did the losing team have?_____

Relief Pitchers

Use the worksheet titled "Relief Pitchers" on page 25 for this activity. Students will explore how big a role relief pitchers have in baseball games. Hold the draft as explained in the introduction to assign games to students. Each student will record pitching statistics for a major league baseball game. Give each participating student a copy of the worksheet. One or more students can participate.

Each student will find his or her box score in the sports page. Each baseball box score is comprised of two sections. There is a section for batting statistics and a section for pitching statistics. The section for pitchers lists all the pitchers who entered the game for each team. First, have students find the starting pitcher. This is accomplished by reading the game schedule from the day before or by reading the article about that game. Record the information for the two starting pitchers from each team in the spaces provided on the worksheet. Then find the number of innings that the relief pitchers from each team threw. Do not itemize the number of relief pitchers used in the game like the statistics in the paper. Simply write down the number of innings that the starting pitchers did not pitch. At the bottom of the worksheet, write the totals.

Each student will be accountable for 18 innings pitched per game (nine innings for each team). After students complete the worksheets, draw a line on the board (or use an overhead projector) to make two columns. One column should be labeled "Starting Pitchers" and the other column should be labeled "Relief Pitchers." Have students volunteer their information as you record it on the board. Have students tell you how many innings their starting pitchers threw for and how many innings their relief pitchers threw for. Total the results upon completion. Discuss which pitchers threw for the most innings. If you desire, have students tell which percent of the innings starting pitchers threw for. This is accomplished by dividing the total number of innings pitched by the number of innings the starting pitchers threw for. Then, simply change that decimal into a percent.

Baseball Predictions

Use the worksheet titled "Baseball Predictions" on page 26 for this activity. Using a major league schedule from the sports page, the teacher will fill in the games on the blank worksheet before making copies and handing them out to the participating students. Try to use this activity when there is a full slate of games. You may wish to give the worksheet to students on a Friday afternoon during baseball season and use the games that occur over the weekend.

Students will circle the team that they think will win each game. They will also write in the total number of runs that they think will be scored during the game. When students return to class the next day, pass the sports page to each participating member of the class. Have class members see how many games they predicted correctly. Have students write the actual total score in the space provided to see if they matched any games exactly.

Relief Pitchers

Opponents: _____ vs. _____

Home Team: _____

Number of innings pitched by the starting pitcher _____

Number of innings pitched by the relief pitcher(s) _____

Visiting Team: _____

Number of innings pitched by the starting pitcher _____

Number of innings pitched by the relief pitcher(s) _____

Totals

Number of innings pitched by the starting pitchers _____

Number of innings pitched by the relief pitchers _____

Baseball Predictions

Circle the team that you think will win the game. In the space provided, write how many points you think both teams will score.

Visiting Team	Home Team	Predicted Runs	Actual Runs

How many games did you predict correctly?_____

Did you guess any of the total scores correctly?_____ If so, how many?_____

Computing Batting Averages

Ask students what it means when an announcer at a baseball game states that a player is batting .341. Most students will know that it is the batting average of a player. Many students, however, will not know how statisticians arrive at those numbers.

In this activity, students will find out how batting averages are computed. Students will need a background in changing fractions to decimals. Begin by having each participant choose a major league baseball player that is not a pitcher or designated hitter—the player must be in the starting lineup. Hand out the worksheet titled "Computing Batting Averages" on page 28.

Students will follow their players for a total of 10 games, studying the results of each game in the box scores. They will record data in the space provided on their worksheets. Direct students to the box score section of the sports page. There, students will find the results of their players' performances from the previous day.

Students will need to gather information from two particular columns on the box score. The headings of those two columns will be labeled **AB** and **H**. The **AB** heading means "At Bats." This statistic tells how many times the player *officially* went to bat during that game. (Walks and sacrifices, for instance, don't count as official "at bats.") The **H** heading tells how many hits the player had during that game. Have students use the appropriate space on the worksheet to record this data for each of 10 games. Remember that teams do not play every day. There may be an interval of one to three days between games. This activity may take up to two weeks of classtime to record data.

After students have completed gathering their data for the 10 games, have them refer to the bottom of the worksheet. Add the totals for hits and at bats for the 10 games and write the numbers in the spaces provided. The formula to compute batting average is number of *hits* divided by *times at bat* equals *batting average* (**h ÷ ab = ba**). To compute this formula, have students make a fraction in the space provided. The number of hits will be the numerator. The times at bat will be the denominator.

At this point, review with students how to change a fraction to a decimal. You may wish to allow students to use a calculator for this operation. The first three numbers comprise the batting average of the player. **Note:** If the fourth number is a 5 or larger, the batting average is rounded up (i.e., 1 is added to the third number). For example, .3235 would round up to .324; whereas, .3234 would remain .323.

> **Kirby Puckett**
>
> **AB**   **H**
> 657   234
>
> Formula:
> **Hits** divided by **At Bats**
>
> H/AB = 234/657
> 234/657 = .35616438356
>
> Batting Average: .356

Have students compare the average for the 10 games to the season average of the player. They will find the season average of baseball players in the sports page once per week, usually in a Wednesday or Thursday edition.

Computing Batting Averages

Player's name _____

Game Number	Times At Bat	Number of Hits
Game 1		
Game 2		
Game 3		
Game 4		
Game 5		
Game 6		
Game 7		
Game 8		
Game 9		
Game 10		

Total Number of Hits	Total Times At Bat	Fraction or Hits divided by At Bats

Batting Average _____

Major League Baseball Attendance

Find the worksheet titled "Major League Baseball Attendance" on page 30 for this activity. You will need to have access to a sports page for five consecutive days during baseball's regular season. This activity will work well for any number of participants.

Students will chart daily attendance at major league baseball games for five days and find the average attendance for each day. Have students look at the box-score section of the sports page on Monday. At the bottom of each individual box score, there will be an attendance figure for each game. Find all the attendance figures for the major league games played on that day. Write those figures in the boxes under the Monday section of the worksheet. Have students add all the boxes and divide by the number of boxes that were filled. This will give you the average attendance for one day. Write that figure in the space provided under the Monday section of the worksheet.

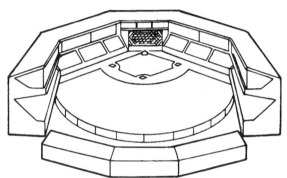

Continue in this manner for each day of the week. Then add the daily averages together. This will give you the average weekly baseball attendance.

As an extension to this activity, have students estimate how many people might watch games on the other two days of the week that were not accounted for (Friday and Saturday). Add this figure to your daily attendance sum and recalculate the average, this time dividing the number by seven.

Baseball Runs by the Inning

Find out in which innings baseball players score the most runs. Use the tally sheet titled "Baseball Runs by the Inning" on page 31 for this activity. Find line scores of baseball games in the sports page. Use professional games, high school games, or softball games. Be sure that the games are nine-inning contests.

On the worksheet, have students make a tally for each run under the appropriate inning. You may wish to give students more than one copy of the worksheet to track different levels of play. For example, one worksheet would be labeled professional runs, another would be labeled college runs, etc. Track the number of runs for a given number of days, perhaps 2–3 days. In the space provided by each inning box, write the number of runs that baseball teams scored each inning.

Write the results on the board or on the overhead projector. Ask students to explain the distribution of runs. Why did some innings produce more runs than others? You may also wish to have students make a simple bar graph of their results.

Major League Baseball Attendance

Monday Attendance

Monday's average attendance _____

Tuesday Attendance

Tuesday's average attendance _____

Wednesday Attendance

Wednesday's average attendance _____

Thursday Attendance

Thursday's average attendance _____

Friday Attendance

Friday's average attendance _____

Write the weekly average here _____

Baseball Runs by the Inning

Inning	Runs scored
First	
Second	
Third	
Fourth	
Fifth	
Sixth	
Seventh	
Eighth	
Ninth	

First inning runs _____

Second inning runs _____

Third inning runs _____

Fourth inning runs _____

Fifth inning runs _____

Sixth inning runs _____

Seventh inning runs _____

Eighth inning runs _____

Ninth inning runs _____

Challenge: If you combine innings 1–9, how many total runs were scored?

Sports Page Trivia: Baseball

To play "Sports Page Trivia: Baseball," the teacher will divide the class into two teams. If the entire class does not wish to participate, the activity will work equally well with smaller groups or even one player against another. Each team will need a copy of the worksheet titled "Sports Page Trivia: Baseball" on page 33. Each team member will also need a copy of the worksheet titled "Activity Cards" on page 142. You will also need two separate sports pages. They must be identical—from the same day and same publication.

First, have the teams each find a place to meet in the room. Each team will look through the sports page and find questions to present to the other team. Encourage students not to find questions that are too difficult to answer, such as "How many people were at the Astros vs. Braves game last night?" "Who won the Yankees vs. Red Sox game?" is an appropriate question. Inform students that you are the referee and inappropriate questions may result in a penalty. Have students record the questions on the activity cards and cut them out. Students should also write the correct answer to the question on the back of the card. Remember that all the questions should be related to baseball.

Now students are ready to begin the competition. Each team should have its copy of the baseball diamond on the worksheet. The teams will also need pennies or other markers. Start by allowing Team 1 to ask Team 2 a question. If Team 2 is able to answer the question correctly, they are allowed to send a "runner" to first base. If they are unable to answer the question correctly, there is one out. Continue with the next question. If Team 2 answers two consecutive questions correctly, they will have runners on first and second base. If Team 1 asks three questions that Team 2 is unable to answer, then it is time for Team 1 to go to bat. At this point, Team 2 will ask questions to Team 1.

Inning	1	2	3	4	5	6	7	8	9 — Final
Team 1	1	0	0	3	2	1	2	2	3 — 14
Team 2	0	2	1	0	3	4	0	1	2 — 13

The game will proceed in this manner until nine innings are completed. The team that was able to get the most runners across home plate is the winner. The teacher may act as the umpire to determine if questions are fair. A student who does not wish to participate may want to be the scorekeeper at the board, keeping track of innings and runs.

Sports Page Trivia: Baseball

Third Base

Second Base

Home Plate

First Base

Home Run Kings

The home run is the most dramatic play in baseball. It can change the outcome of a game in a split second. Make a bulletin board titled "Home Run Kings." This activity will work best if it is started at the beginning of the baseball season. List the name of each major league team on 3" x 7" (8 cm x 18 cm) pieces of construction paper or tagboard. Allow students to decorate the team nametags, using logos of teams from the sports page or sports magazines.

Assign each student in the class a baseball team or use the draft as explained in the introduction to let students choose their own teams. Each student will follow a baseball team on a daily basis and keep track of the players that hit the most home runs. Give each student a copy of the worksheet titled "Activity Cards" on page 142. Individual home runs are listed in the box score section of the sports page. The letters "HR" underneath the batting statistics for each game designates them. Each player who hits a home run in that game is listed, and the number in parentheses next to the player's name tells how many home runs that player has hit for the season thus far.

When a player on his or her team hits a home run, have the student write down that player's name on an activity card and place it under his or her team name on the bulletin board. After a few weeks, look at the board to see which teams and players have the most home runs.

RBI Race

RBI (runs batted in) is a term used in baseball to mean the number of base runners a batter hits across home plate. For example, if a runner is on second base and a batter comes to the plate and hits a double, the runner on second base would most likely score. If the runner does score, the batter that hit the double would be credited with an RBI. A player is also credited for getting him or herself across the plate when a home run is hit. For this activity, students will follow a team and use the player that hit the most RBI each game to see how far they can travel across a graph. Give each student a copy of the worksheet "RBI Race" on page 35.

Have students choose teams using the draft as described in the introduction. Students will each have five games to get their RBI totals. For each of the five games, students will look in the box score section on the sports page and find the players on their teams that had the most RBI for that game. RBI are found in the batting statistics for individual players designated by the letters **RBI** or **BI**. List the name of the player and the number of RBI that he hit for each game in the chart at the top of the worksheet. Then shade in the number along the graph at the bottom of the worksheet. The student with the most RBI at the end of the five-game period will win the contest. The game probably will not end on the same day, as the baseball schedule will differ for each team.

(**Note:** Until as recently as the 1990s, sportswriters and sportscasters alike often used the term "RBIs" to denote the plural form of "RBI." [For example: "Puckett collected six RBIs in last night's game."] However, since "RBIs" literally translates to the awkward "run batted ins," the sports community now considers "RBI" to be the correct term for both the singular and plural forms of the abbreviation.)

RBI Race

Team Name_____

List the team's RBI leader for each of the next five games.

	Team Leader in RBI	Number of RBI
Game 1		
Game 2		
Game 3		
Game 4		
Game 5		

Use markers or colored pencils to graph the progress of your team's RBI leader each day.
Use a different color of marker for each day.

0   5   10   15   20   25   30   35   40

Total RBI for five days_____

Pinch Hitters and Designated Hitters

Major League Baseball is divided into two separate leagues: the National League and the American League. There is one major difference between the rules of the two leagues. In the American League, the pitchers do not have to bat because teams are allowed to use designated hitters for them. This means that the designated hitter plays offense (hits) for the pitcher, who in turn only plays defense (in this case, pitches). (Usually, a team's manager will assign the designated hitter role to someone who is a good hitter but is just not very good at playing defense.) In the National League, however, the pitcher must bat for himself. Sometimes if a manager knows that he will not need the current pitcher in the next inning or if he wants a batter who is a better hitter than that pitcher, he will use a pinch hitter. The pinch hitter takes the place of the pitcher for whom he is hitting in the batting lineup. This means that the pitcher cannot reenter the game—he is ineligible for the rest of the contest. Pinch hitters can be used for position players, also; this is why the American League has pinch hitters, too.

In this activity, students will look at the statistics of designated hitters and pinch hitters. Each participant will need a copy of the worksheet titled "Pinch Hitters and Designated Hitters" on page 37.

Have students refer to the box score section of the paper for this activity. Look at the batting statistics for each game. Go down the list of batters and find the letter symbols for pinch hitters and designated hitters (**PH** and **DH** respectively). Have students record the batting statistics for each player on the worksheet. Fill all the spaces for players on the worksheet, if possible. Total the statistics at the bottom.

Ask students to find the batting averages for the pinch hitters and the designated hitters. This is accomplished by dividing the total number of hits by the total times at bat. Change the decimal to percent form by multiplying times 100 and rounding the decimal to the nearest whole number. Then discuss which league had the best replacement batters for that day. Ask students to find individual batting statistics in the paper. See how the designated hitters and pinch hitters compare to the regular hitters on the teams.

Baseball Boo-Boos

Give students a copy of the worksheet "Baseball Boo-Boos" on page 38 for this activity. Students will keep track of a baseball team's errors for a two-week period and try to find a correlation with that team's win/loss record. This activity will work with one or more students.

Give each student a copy of the worksheet. Students will track the errors made by a team and the players who make them. For each game, have students refer to the box score section of the sports page. Errors are listed under the batting section of the box score for each game. An **E** denotes the errors. The players' names and the number of errors committed are also included.

Have each student follow a team of his or her choice for a 10-game period. Instruct each student to write the information on the worksheet each day that his or her team has a game. After students have filled out the worksheet, have him or her compare it to a classmate's worksheet for a different team. Look at the win/loss records of the teams to find a correlation between win/loss records and the number of errors a team commits. Also, find the player who committed the most errors.

Pinch Hitters and Designated Hitters

Pinch Hitters (National League)

Team	Player	At Bats	Hits	Runs	Runs Batted In

Totals _____ _____ _____ _____

Designated Hitters (American League)

Team	Player	At Bats	Hits	Runs	Runs Batted In

Totals _____ _____ _____ _____

Baseball Boo-Boos

Name of Team _____

Game 1 versus _____

Player				
# of errors				

Game 2 versus _____

Player				
# of errors				

Game 3 versus _____

Player				
# of errors				

Game 4 versus _____

Player				
# of errors				

Game 5 versus _____

Player				
# of errors				

Game 6 versus _____

Player				
# of errors				

Game 7 versus _____

Player				
# of errors				

Game 8 versus _____

Player				
# of errors				

Game 9 versus _____

Player				
# of errors				

Game 10 versus _____

Player				
# of errors				

Sample Football Box Score

Broncos 33, Vikings 30

Denver	10	7	3	13	—	33
Minnesota	7	8	0	15	—	30

FIRST QUARTER

Min—Carter 31 pass from Johnson (Anderson kick) 8:13

Den—FG Elam 44 5:07

Den—Sharpe 11 pass from Elway (Elam kick) 2:22

SECOND QUARTER

Min—Safety, Elway sacked in end zone by Randle 7:35

Den—Davis 16 run (Elam kick) 3:11

Min—Moss 77 pass from Johnson (run failed) 0:52

THIRD QUARTER

Den—FG Elam 37 7:48

FOURTH QUARTER

Den—FG Elam 22 14:44

Min—Palmer 96 kickoff return (Carter pass) 14:32

Den—FG Elam 60 5:55

Min—Carter 13 pass from Johnson (Anderson kick) 1:01

Den—McCaffrey 27 pass from Elway (Elam kick) 0:07

A: 59,213

Team Statistics	Den	Min
First Downs	32	25
Rushes–Yards	35–184	27–137
Passing	275	394
Punt–Ret.Yds.	2–30	3–33
Kickoff–Ret.Yds.	3–62	6–199
Interceptions–Ret.Yds.	1–13	0–0
Comp.–Att.–Int.	22–32–0	32–39–1
Sacked–Yds.Lost	6–32	2–19
Punts–Avg.Yds.	5–41.7	4–46.3
Fumbles–Lost	1–0	2–2
Penalties–Yards	4–25	5–40
Time of Possession	33:34	26:26

Individual Statistics

Rushing: Denver—Davis 27–153; Elway 4–25; Loville 4–6. Minnesota—
Smith 20–101; Hoard 5–22; Palmer 1–8; Moss 1–6.

Passing: Denver—Elway 22–32–0, 307. Minnesota—Johnson 32–39–1, 413.

Receiving: Denver—McCaffrey 8–122; Sharpe 7–69; Davis 4–63; Smith 2–44;
Carswell 1–9. Minnesota—Carter 12–137; Moss 7–113; Reed 4–76;
Glover 3–33; Palmer 2–22; Smith 3–13; Hatchette 1–19.

Missed Field Goals: Minnesota—Anderson 44 (BK)

Football Scavenger Hunt #1

Find the following from the sports page and glue them on your answer sheet.

1. a picture of a football

2. the word *quarterback*

3. the name of a professional football team

4. the word *yards*

5. the name of a professional quarterback

6. a team that scored more than 30 points

7. a team name that is an animal

8. a person who caught a pass

9. the word *penalty*

10. the number of passes a quarterback attempted

Football Scavenger Hunt #2

Find the following from the sports page and glue them on your answer sheet.

1. the name of a stadium

2. the number of first downs a team made

3. a home team

4. a team that plays indoors

5. a city where an NFL game was played

6. a team with blue on their jerseys

7. a team from Florida

8. a player who ran for more than 80 yards

9. a box score from a game

10. a picture of a football helmet

Football Scavenger Hunt #3

Find the following from the sports page and glue them on your answer sheet.

1. a team that plays outdoors

2. the word *completed*

3. a picture of any football player

4. the name of a placekicker

5. an NFL city west of the Mississippi River

6. a team with a losing record

7. a quarterback who threw for more than 250 yards

8. a game that produced more than 60 points

9. a player who was injured during a game

10. the name of a player who intercepted a pass

Football Scavenger Hunt #4

Find the following from the sports page and glue them on your answer sheet.

1. the word *attendance*

2. a player who sacked a quarterback

3. a team name that is a cat

4. a game played on artificial grass

5. the name of a placekicker who scored more than 6 points

6. the number of minutes a team possessed the football

7. a receiver who caught more than 6 passes

8. a team that did not score any points in the fourth quarter

9. a game that was decided by fewer than three points

10. the word *turnovers*

Football Scavenger Hunt #5

Find the following from the sports page and glue them on your answer sheet.

1. a game that totaled fewer than 30 points

2. an NFL city that is on the Great Lakes

3. a football team that is not named after an animal

4. a quarterback who threw for fewer than 200 yards

5. a running back who averaged more than 3 yards per carry

6. a punter who kicked one punt over 45 yards

7. the word *knee* from an article.

8. any defensive player

9. a team that made more than 15 first downs

10. a team that might strike gold

Football Scavenger Hunt #6

Find the following from the sports page and glue them on your answer sheet.

1. a picture of a football fan

2. a team that scored a number of points divisible by 3

3. a quarterback who completed an even number of passes

4. the term *end zone*

5. a picture of a player with a jersey number lower than 50

6. a football team name that describes a huge person

7. a team that has won one more game than it has lost

8. a team that has scored more points than it has given up

9. a placekicker who missed a field goal

10. a team that scored exactly seven points in a quarter

Football Scavenger Hunt #7

Find the following from the sports page and glue them on your answer sheet.

1. a team that plays in a former Confederate state
2. a receiver who averaged more than 15 yards per catch
3. a team that soars above the clouds
4. the word *seconds*
5. an AFC team that played at home

6. a player with a **y** in his name
7. a quarterback who completed under 50 percent of his passes
8. a picture with more than one football player in it
9. an NFC team that played an AFC team
10. a team that plays on natural grass

Football Scavenger Hunt #8

Find the following from the sports page and glue them on your answer sheet.

1. the word *fourth*
2. a home team that lost
3. a team that played a team from the same division
4. a team named after something that might live in the jungle
5. a placekicker who made more than 70 percent of his field goal attempts

6. an NFC team that played a game on artificial grass
7. a player who did not touch the football during the game
8. a player whose last name begins with **S**
9. a game where both teams' scores ended in even digits
10. a player who sacked a quarterback

Football Scavenger Hunt #9

Find the following from the sports page and glue them on your answer sheet.

1. a quarterback who completed more than 60 percent of his passes

2. a team named for people who might live on a ranch

3. a team from an American city that is near the Canadian border

4. an injured player from the AFC

5. last year's Super Bowl Champion

6. a punter who averaged fewer than 40 yards per punt

7. the word *rookie*

8. two teams that combined for first downs divisible by 3

9. a team with a logo on only one side of their helmets

10. a picture of a player with only one foot on the ground

Football Scavenger Hunt #10

Find the following from the sports page and glue them on your answer sheet.

1. a team named for people who have pride in their country

2. a number from the box scores that is a square of another number

3. an attendance number that is divisible by 3

4. a team named after ancient explorers from Scandinavia

5. the phrase *#1 draft pick*

6. a picture of someone on the sidelines

7. a team named for a mammel that lives in the water

8. the word *dropped*

9. a team whose name does not have a long vowel sound

10. the total score of a game that ended in a number that is a multiple of 4

Football Fun

Beginner

Use this activity on Friday afternoon. Each student will get to choose a quarterback, a running back, a receiver, and a place kicker from NFL teams. You may find it useful to have a copy of the sports page from last Monday. This paper will have the box scores for the NFL games from the prior Sunday. This will give students a list of all the players from which to choose. This activity will work with two or more players. Not all class members have to participate.

Use the draft as explained in the introduction of the workbook. Give students a copy of the worksheet titled "Football Fun (Beginner)" on page 46. After the draft, have the student chosen number one in the draft pick a quarterback and list him on his or her sheet in the appropriate place. Then have the player selected number two in the draft make a selection for quarterback and record his or her selection on the worksheet. Continue this process until all participants have chosen a quarterback.

Hold the draft again. This time have each player select a running back from NFL teams. Record the name of the running back in the appropriate place on the worksheet. If students desire, they may choose a quarterback and a running back from the same team. Students are also allowed to choose quarterbacks, running backs, receivers, and placekickers from different teams.

Continue this process until each player has one player for each of the four positions. Make sure students record their players in the appropriate places on the worksheet. You may wish to discourage students from choosing players from the two teams that play on Monday Night Football. This way students will be able to tally their results on Monday instead of having to wait until Tuesday. Some students may wish to take their sheets home and keep track of their choices during the games on Sunday. Advise these students to make copies of their worksheets to take home; have them leave the originals at school.

```
My Team

QB: Peyton Manning

RB: Terrell Davis

WR: Cris Carter

K: Morten Andersen
```

On the following Monday, have copies of the sports page in the classroom. At any point in the day, you may wish to go over the results as a class. The teacher may also pass the sports page around the room and have students find results individually. Use the system below to tally points.

Look at the box score of each game that is pertinent to individual students. Advise students to find their quarterbacks first. If the quarterback ran or threw for touchdowns, the student will get six points for each score. Next, students will tally the number of touchdowns that their running back scored and record six points for each. Continue this process for the receivers, giving six points for each touchdown scored. For the place kickers, students will receive three points for each field goal and one point for each point after a touchdown.

After students have tallied all their points, add the totals for each of their four players. The winner is the student with the highest total points.

Football Fun

Beginner *(cont.)*

Quarterback	Team	Touchdowns	Points

Running Back	Team	Touchdowns	Points

Receiver	Team	Touchdowns	Points

Placekicker	Team	Field Goals	Extra Points	Total Points

Total Points from all four players _____

Football Fun

Expert

"Football Fun (Expert)" is designed for students with advanced skill levels. Each participating student will need a copy of the worksheet titled "Football Fun (Expert)" on page 48. This activity may be used as a class activity, or any number of individual students may participate.

Use this activity on a Friday afternoon on any week of the NFL season. It may be useful to have a copy of a sports page from the previous Monday. The box scores will help students with their choices of players. Hold the draft as explained in the introduction. Students will track the progress of players for a period of five weeks. On Mondays, students will tally data to determine their points.

After the initial draft, have students choose their quarterbacks and record them in the appropriate place on the worksheet. Hold the draft again and have students choose their running backs. Continue this process until all positions on the worksheet are filled.

Be sure to have Monday's sports page in the classroom when students return from the weekend. Students will use the box scores to record data on their worksheets. Use the following system to determine total points.

Quarterbacks:
- gain 1 point for each completion they throw
- gain 6 points for each touchdown they score
- lose 1 point for each incomplete pass they throw
- lose 2 points for each interception they throw

Running Backs:
- gain 1 point for each catch
- gain 1 point for each increment of 20 yards they gain during the game
- gain 6 points for each touchdown they score

Receivers:
- gain 1 point for each catch
- gain 1 point for each increment of 20 yards they gain during the game
- gain 6 points for each touchdown they score

Placekickers:
- gain 3 points for each successful field goal attempt
- gain 1 point for each successful extra point attempt

Tally the total points on students' worksheets to determine the winner!

Football Fun

Expert *(cont.)*

Quarterback _____ **Team** _____

completed passes (1)	incomplete passes (-1)	touchdowns (6)	interceptions (-2)

Total points quarterback_____

Running Back _____ **Team** _____

number of catches (1)	every 20 yards (1)	touchdowns (6)

Total points running back_____

Receiver_____ **Team**_____

number of catches (1)	every 20 yards (1)	touchdowns (6)

Total points receiver_____

Placekicker _____ **Team** _____

field goals (3)	extra points (1)

Total points placekicker_____

Total points for all four players_____

NFL Football Name Fun

Find professional football teams in the sports page that fit the descriptions below. Cut their names from the newspaper and glue them in the spaces provided.

1. This team might live on a ranch. _____

2. This team is always looking for gold. _____

3. This team might say "Fee Fi Fo Fum." _____

4. This team can soar above the clouds. _____

5. This team is too young to buck you off. _____

6. This team's members are strong swimmers. _____

7. This team lets out a mighty roar. _____

8. This team might have cubs. _____

9. You might see this team at the airport. _____

10. This team is proud to be American. _____

11. Beige, tan, and ecru belong on this team. _____

12. You wouldn't want to hit heads with this team. _____

13. This team is always well behaved. _____

Teacher Note: Fold answers under before photocopying this page for students.

Answers

1. Cowboys 2. 49ers 3. Giants 4. Eagles, Ravens, Cardinals, Falcons 5. Colts 6. Dolphins 7. Lions
8. Bears 9. Jets 10. Patriots 11. Browns 12. Rams 13. Saints

Super Bowl Fun

Pre-game

Read the sports page the week before the Super Bowl to help you find answers to the following questions about the two teams competing in the big game.

1. At what stadium will the game be played? _____

2. What is the capacity of the stadium? _____

3. Which team is the underdog? _____

4. Find the average weight of the NFC team's starting offensive linemen. _____

5. Using the players on this year's Super Bowl rosters, which college did the most athletes attend before they became professional football players?

   _____

6. Which television network will broadcast the Super Bowl? _____

7. How much will advertisers pay to televise a commercial during the Super Bowl?

   _____

8. Try to find a player who has played for both of the Super Bowl teams. _____

   _____

9. What is the Roman numeral for this year's Super Bowl? _____

10. Name an injured player who will not play in the game.

   _____

11. Which defense gave up the lesser number of total yards this season?

   _____

12. Which running back gained the most yards this season? _____

13. Which receiver caught the most passes this season? _____

14. Which team won its conference championship game by more points?

   _____

15. Which player has the highest number on his uniform? _____

Super Bowl Fun *(cont.)*

Game Day

Fill out this activity sheet the Friday before the Super Bowl. Have the sheet handy as you watch the game to see if you are correct. Do not change your answers after the game has begun. If you answer a question correctly, give yourself the number of points in parentheses next to it. Total your points at the bottom of the page.

1. Name the team that will receive the opening kickoff. _____ (3)

2. Name the player you think will score the first touchdown.
   _____ (10)

3. What do you think the first penalty in the game will be?
   _____ (5)

4. Name the team that will call the first time-out. _____ (3)

5. Name the team that will punt first. _____ (3)

6. Name the team that will cross the opponent's 50-yard line
   first. _____ (3)

7. Name the kicker who will kick the first field goal. _____ (3)

8. Which player will be first to intercept a pass? _____ (10)

9. Name the total number of points that will be scored by both
   teams. _____ _____(10)

10. Name the team that will have the ball when the game ends. _____ (3)

11. What do you think the final point difference will be? _____ (5)

12. Name the team that will win the game. _____ (5)

Total points _____

Super Bowl Fun *(cont.)*

Post-game

Use the sports page the day after the Super Bowl to find answers to the following questions.

1. Find a receiver who caught at least five passes during the Super Bowl.

   _____

2. Name the running back who gained the most yards. _____

3. What was the biggest lead by either team? _____

4. How many lead changes occurred during the Super Bowl? _____

5. Which quarterback threw the most passes? _____

6. Which quarterback threw for the most yards? _____

7. How many turnovers occurred during the Super Bowl? _____

8. Which team punted the most? _____

9. Did either team or any individual player break any Super Bowl records?
   _____ If so, name one. _____

10. Who was the game's leading tackler? _____

11. How many interceptions were thrown during the Super Bowl? _____

12. Which team committed the most penalties? _____
    For how many yards was this team penalized? _____

13. Which team allowed the fewest yards from scrimmage? _____

14. Which team made the most first downs? _____

15. What was the longest field goal kicked during the game? _____

NFL Quarterbacks

Use the worksheet titled "NFL Quarterbacks" on page 54 for this activity. This activity can be used with an entire class or with a small group of individuals. If fewer than five students are participating, allow students to choose their own quarterbacks. If more than five students participate, you may wish to hold the draft to compare more quarterbacks. This activity will be most successful if four or more students participate.

Have students choose an NFL quarterback at any point in the season. After each game, have students compile the statistics required on the worksheet. Use statistics from the box scores to acquire the needed information. Monday sports pages will have weekly NFL box scores. Students should track the progress of their quarterbacks for five consecutive weeks during the season. After five weeks, students will need to do the arithmetic to find the percent form of pass completions and yards per pass.

To find the percentage of completed passes, simply divide the number of completed passes by the number of passes attempted. Allow students to use a calculator for these operations. Round the decimal to the nearest thousandth. Then multiply that number by 100 or move the decimal two places to the right. Round the new number to the nearest percent.

To find the average number of yards per completion, divide the number of yards by the number of completed passes. Round this figure to the nearest whole number. At this time, total the number of touchdown passes and the number of interceptions in the appropriate columns.

After students finish the operations above, divide the class into four groups. Each group will need colored markers and a large piece of white paper on which to draw graphs. Assign each group one of the following categories and have it label its graphs for identification: Completion Percentage of Passes Thrown, Average Yards Per Completion, Touchdowns, and Interceptions. Now list all of the quarterbacks vertically down the graphs. Make sure that each group lists the quarterbacks in the same order.

Next, have students graph their results in bar graph format. The group working on the graph titled "Completion Percentage of Passes Thrown" will use numbers from 0–100 on their horizontal axis. The group working on the graph titled "Average Yards Per Completion" will use numbers 0–40 on their horizontal axis. The groups working on the graphs titled "Touchdowns" and "Interceptions" will number their horizontal axes from 0–50.

Students will use the markers to graph information for each quarterback, using the activity sheet. After students have finished the graphs, hang them in a spot visible to all members of the class. Discuss the graphs with your class. At this time, have a copy of each team's won/loss record for discussion. Examine the ratio between interceptions and touchdowns. Which quarterback has the best ratio? Find the quarterback who averages the most yards per attempt. Look at the records of the teams for each quarterback. Do the teams that win the most always have the quarterbacks who perform the best?

NFL Quarterbacks

Name of Quarterback _____

	Passes Attempted	Passes Completed	Touchdowns	Interceptions
Game 1				
Game 2				
Game 3				
Game 4				
Game 5				

Add the columns from each of the five weeks and record the totals in the spaces below.

	Passes Attempted	Passes Completed	Touchdowns	Interceptions
Totals:				

NFL Running Backs

You will need the worksheet titled "NFL Running Backs" on page 56 for this activity. Students will chart the progress of their chosen running backs for the NFL season. The activity works best if students begin collecting data from the first week of the season until the end of the season, collecting data for all 16 weeks. The activity will work equally well with one student or an entire class.

You may wish to use the draft to assign running backs to students so that the less popular running backs are considered as well. Students will need to refer to the box scores each Monday of the NFL season to find information about their running backs. Each student will need a copy of the worksheet. Record the information in the boxes provided on the worksheet each week.

At the completion of the NFL season, students will construct broken-line graphs. A broken-line graph gives information over a period of time. Use a large piece of butcher paper for the graphs. The paper should have a vertical boundary of one foot and a horizontal boundary of three feet. Draw axis lines on the paper about six inches inside the edge of each paper as seen in the example below.

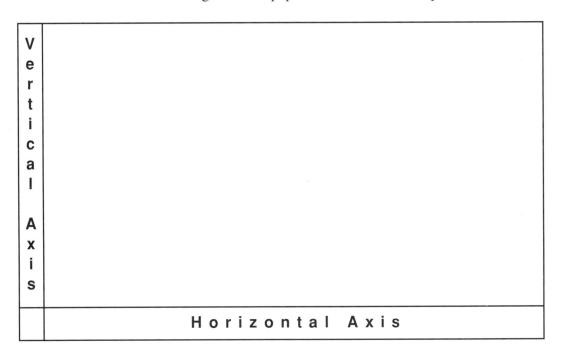

Be sure to label the graph by the name of the player. Divide the horizontal axis into 16 even sections and label them for each week of the season, starting with week 1. Label the vertical axis as yards per game. The numbering for the vertical axis should go from 0–300 in even increments. Have students place a dot on each week of the season for how many yards their player rushed. For example, if a player ran for 138 yards during the first week of the season, the students would align 138 on the vertical axis with the week 1 point on the horizontal axis and place the dot. Do this for each week of the season. Connect the dots to evaluate the player's performance.

You may wish to divide the class into groups and make different broken-line graphs. From the information on the worksheet, you can construct graphs for yards per carry, rushing attempts per game, touchdowns, or fumbles per game, as well.

Have students look at their social studies books to find other examples of broken line graphs. Discuss similarities and differences among the graphs you made.

NFL Running Backs

Name of Running Back _____

	Rushing Attempts	Yards Gained	Touchdowns	Fumbles
Game 1				
Game 2				
Game 3				
Game 4				
Game 5				
Game 6				
Game 7				
Game 8				
Game 9				
Game 10				
Game 11				
Game 12				
Game 13				
Game 14				
Game 15				
Game 16				

Totals:

Yards per game = total yards divided by total number of games (16) _____

Yards per carry = total number of yards divided by total number of carries _____

NFL Receivers

For this activity, you will need a copy of the worksheet titled "NFL Receivers Sign-Up" on page 58. Give each student a copy of the worksheet.

Hold the draft as described in the introduction to determine the order of choosing the receivers. Each student will get to choose a receiver from the NFL. Allow students to choose receivers from teams that have already had a receiver chosen. For example, if a student chooses a receiver from the Oakland Raiders, another receiver from the Raiders may be picked, also.

Pass around the sign-up worksheet as students are seated at their desks. With the worksheet, pass around copies of the Monday sports page during the NFL season. Students will each list the receiver of choice and the team for which he plays, as well as their own names. Remember that students may choose more than one receiver from each NFL team. Be sure to have students choose in the order that they were assigned in the draft.

NFL Receiver Draft
1. C. Carter, Min.
2. Rice, SF
3. Hutson, GB
4. Alworth, SD
5. Swann, Pit.
6. Taylor, Wash.
7. Largent, Sea.
8. Biletnikoff, Oak.
9. Hirsch, LA
10. Sharpe, GB

When students have finished filling out the worksheet with their receivers, make a photocopy in case you want to use the activity for more than one week. After the weekend games, pass the sheet and the Monday sports page around again and have students list the information about their receivers. This information can be found in the box scores. They will need to write in the number of receptions, the number of yards, and the number of touchdowns that each receiver made. Examine the results with the class. Ask students to find how many yards his or her receiver averaged by dividing the number of yards by the number of receptions. Find out which player had the most total yards and which player made the most touchdowns. Find a correlation between winning teams and the performance of their receivers. Did any receivers who gained many yards play on teams that lost?

NFL Receivers Sign-Up

Student	Receiver	Team	Rec.	Yds.	TDs

Legend

Rec. = Receptions   Yds. = Yards   TDs = Touchdowns

Football Thieves

Students will construct their own bulletin board to find out who leads the NFL in takeaways. Have students cut out the words "Football Thieves" in two-inch stencil and put these words at the top of the bulletin board. Then have students write the name of each NFL team on activity cards from the worksheet on page 142. Place the names across the top of your bulletin board. Cut up more activity cards and have them handy for each week that you wish to track the progress of turnovers.

Use the sports page to find out who made interceptions, fumble recoveries, blocked punts, or blocked field goals. Write the player's name on a card and put it under the team for which he plays. Also list on the card the kind of turnover the player caused. If a player intercepted two passes, he would get two cards under his team's name.

Oakland Raiders

Charles Woodson

Interception

Track turnovers for at least three weeks. Examine the teams that force many turnovers. Do they usually have winning records? Look at the teams that have few turnovers under their names. How do the win/loss records of these teams compare? Allow students to track turnovers until the board is full.

Best and Worst Offenses and Defenses

For this activity, you will need to find a copy of the team statistics in the sports page. This is usually located in a Wednesday or Thursday sports page. Students will look at match ups and predict the results based on a team's standings in the weekly statistics.

Give participating students a copy of the worksheet titled "Best and Worst Offenses and Defenses" on page 60. Have students study the team statistics. On the worksheet, students will list the best five offenses from each conference, the worst five defenses from each conference, the best five defenses from each conference, and the worst five offenses from each conference.

Now look at a schedule for the upcoming weekend. Find the matches that have the greatest discrepancy in rankings and list the games in the spaces provided. For example, the number two offense in the NFC may be playing a number fourteen defense from the AFC. This game and other games will be listed in the spaces on the bottom of the worksheet. Only list the games where a large difference in ranking exists.

Have students study the statistics of these teams before making predictions. Make sure students guess the number of points that each team will score, as well. On Monday, check the results to see if the teams' rankings in the weekly statistics held true. Check to see if a good defense gave up more points than it was supposed to. Maybe a powerful offense did not score at the rate it was accustomed to. Check to see if any of your students guessed a game's point total exactly.

Best and Worst Offenses and Defenses

American Football Conference

Best Offenses
1. _____
2. _____
3. _____
4. _____
5. _____

Worst Defenses
5. _____
4. _____
3. _____
2. _____
1. _____

Best Defenses
1. _____
2. _____
3. _____
4. _____
5. _____

Worst Offenses
5. _____
4. _____
3. _____
2. _____
1. _____

National Football Conference

Best Offenses
1. _____
2. _____
3. _____
4. _____
5. _____

Worst Defenses
5. _____
4. _____
3. _____
2. _____
1. _____

Best Defenses
1. _____
2. _____
3. _____
4. _____
5. _____

Worst Offenses
5. _____
4. _____
3. _____
2. _____
1. _____

Find at least three games where a highly rated offense plays a poorly rated defense or vice versa and predict the outcome below.

Game   Score

_____   _____

_____   _____

_____   _____

Common Football Injuries

Each week the NFL publishes an injury report before the games. Teams list players and the types of injuries sustained. This report is usually found in the sports page on Thursday or Friday during the NFL season. You will need to find the injury report for at least six weeks during the season.

Students will construct a graph to find which injuries are the most common and which occur less frequently. Use a large piece of white butcher paper. The paper should measure two feet (61 cm) in length and three feet (91 cm) in width. Make a horizontal axis and a vertical axis. List injury types along the vertical axis. Make a number scale along the horizontal axis. The number scale should range from 1–20 in even increments.

As injuries occur, list them on the vertical axis. Use a bar graph format to move along the horizontal axis. Each injury of the same type will move the bar further along the horizontal axis. Keep track of the injuries for at least six weeks. Be sure not to add players' injuries to the graph more than once. For example, a player may suffer from a separated shoulder, and he may be listed for more than one week on the injury list. The player should be counted on the graph only once.

NFL Attendance

For this activity, you will need Monday's edition of a sports page each week during the NFL season. Students will keep track of teams' attendance at their home stadiums for the season.

Give each student a copy of the worksheet titled "NFL Attendance" on page 62. At the top of the worksheet, have students list five teams of their choice. To find attendance at NFL games, refer to the box score section of the sports page. At the bottom of each box score, the attendance of that game is listed. Some publications write the word *Attendance*, while others simply employ a capital **A**.

Each NFL team plays eight home games and eight away games during the regular season. For this activity, have students record only the attendance of their teams' home games in the eight spaces provided on the worksheet below the names of the teams. As a class, try to make sure that all NFL teams are accounted for. You may wish to allow students to choose three of their favorite teams and assign the other two teams for each student.

At the conclusion of the season, use classtime to discuss the results. Have students average their results for each team and make a chart or graph. Discuss the correlation between teams' win/loss records and attendance. Discuss stadium attendance by geographic region.

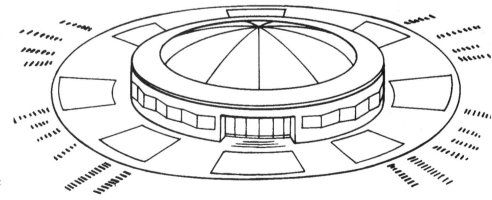

NFL Attendance

Team 1 _____

Team 2 _____

Team 3 _____

Team 4 _____

Team 5 _____

	Team 1	Team 2	Team 3	Team 4	Team 5
Game 1					
Game 2					
Game 3					
Game 4					
Game 5					
Game 6					
Game 7					
Game 8					

Sports Page Trivia: Football

To play "Sports Page Trivia: Football," divide the class into two groups. The entire class does not need to participate. Try to have an even number of students on each team. Each team will have a copy of the worksheet titled "Sports Page Trivia: Football" on page 64. Each team member will also need a copy of the worksheet "Activity Cards" on page 142. You will also need two separate sports pages, one for each team. The sports pages should be identical, from the same publication and the same day. A Monday sports page during football season is best.

First, have the teams find a meeting place to study their sports pages. Students will try to find questions related to football that will stump the other team. Suggest to students that unrealistic questions may result in loss of turn determined by the referee (teacher). An example of such a question is "How many points were scored in all the football games yesterday?" An appropriate question may be "Which team scored the most points yesterday?" Each team will record their questions on the activity cards and cut them out. Be sure to have students write the correct answers on the backs of the cards so that they do not forget them when quizzing the other team. Before a team answers a question, allow the group to huddle and make a group decision before stating an answer. This will avoid confusion for both teams.

Have students refer to the football field on the worksheet. You will need to provide a marker to keep track of yardage. Toss a coin to see who will get possession of the ball first. Put the marker on the 20-yard line. The team in possession will start their drive at this point. They must travel to the opponent's end zone (80 yards) to score a touchdown.

Teams gain yardage by answering questions correctly. For each correctly answered question, the offensive team moves 10 yards. If a team answers four questions incorrectly, they must either kick a field goal or punt.

If the team decides to punt, their opponent gets possession of the ball at their own 20-yard line. A team must be within 40 yards of the opponent's end zone to attempt a field goal. To attempt a field goal, the defensive team asks a question. If the offensive team answers correctly, the field goal attempt is successful. A team scores a touchdown by gaining enough yards to cross the opponent's goal line before they answer four questions incorrectly. In the event of a touchdown, the extra point is contested in the same manner as a field goal. Keep score the same as an actual football game. A touchdown is worth six points, the extra point is worth one point, and a field goal is worth three points.

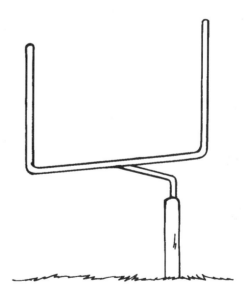

You may wish to put a time limit on the game. Using the clock in the classroom, inform students that the game will end after an allotted number of minutes. You may wish to allow a student who does not want to compete to keep scores on the board.

Sports Page Trivia: Football

END ZONE

-10-

-20-

-30-

-40-

-50-

-40-

-30-

-20-

-10-

END ZONE

NFL Pro Bowl

The Pro Bowl is played in Hawaii at the conclusion of each NFL season. One team's players are selected from the National Football Conference, and the other's are selected from the American Football Conference. These players represent the best performers in the league for the year. Each position on the team is filled with starters and back-up players. The starters are referred to as first-team players, while the backup players are referred to as second-team players.

For this activity, students will need a copy of the worksheet titled "NFL Pro Bowl" on page 66. Hand out two copies of the worksheet to participating students after week 10 of the NFL season. Students will have one month to complete the activity. The teacher will collect the worksheets at the completion of week twelve of the NFL season.

Students will predict who the starting (first team) players for both the NFC and the AFC will be. They will select an offense, a defense, and special teams players from both conferences. (Special teams players include placekickers, punters, kick returners, punt returners, and those who defend against kick and punt returns.) Players' names and team names will be listed in the appropriate spot on the worksheet. Encourage students to use the entire four weeks to make their selections. Students should try to be impartial when making selections, even if they are not fans of the players or teams they may select. Studying the statistics and box scores from the sports page will be beneficial.

Read the sports page each day after the Super Bowl. The Pro Bowl roster will appear during this time. Find the roster in the paper, enlarge it, and give copies to each class member. At this time, hand back students' copies of the worksheet "NFL Pro Bowl" that was previously completed. Have students circle the selections that they correctly chose as first-team members. You may decide to devise a point system to score the papers. Make each correct choice to the first team worth five points and each correct choice to the second team worth two points.

NFL Predictions

Use the worksheet titled "NFL Predictions" on page 67 for this activity. Have the NFL schedule handy to help you fill out the form before you copy and hand it to students. A Friday sports page should have all the NFL games for the coming weekend. Write in the week of the NFL season and fill in each of the fifteen games. Make copies after you have completed the form and give the copies to students on Friday. Students will simply predict who they think will win each of the games played on Sunday and Monday nights and write their predictions in the space provided. Collect the forms before students leave for the weekend. The winner is the student who predicted the most games correctly. If a tie occurs, use the total number of points scored on the Monday night game as the tiebreaker. (In other words, if Denver beats Oakland 27–21 on Monday night, the total points for that game would be 48.)

NFL Pro Bowl

Circle **AFC** or **NFC** .

Offense	Defense
Offense	**Defense**
QB _____	S _____
RB_____	S _____
RB_____	CB_____
WR _____	CB_____
WR _____	LB _____
TE_____	LB _____
OT_____	LB _____
OT_____	DL_____
OG _____	DL_____
OG _____	DL_____
C_____	DL_____
PK_____	P _____

NFL Predictions

	Home Team	Visiting Team	Predicted Winner
Game 1			
Game 2			
Game 3			
Game 4			
Game 5			
Game 6			
Game 7			
Game 8			
Game 9			
Game 10			
Game 11			
Game 12			
Game 13			
Game 14			
Monday Game			

Predict the total number of points that both teams will
score during the Monday Night Football game. _____

Top 25 Colleges vs. the Pros

In this activity, students will pit college teams against pro teams in imaginary games and track the outcomes. You will need the corresponding worksheet on page 69 and the worksheet titled "Activity Cards" on page 142.

Make two copies of the activity cards and cut along the lines. Find a listing of the top 25 college teams in the nation from a sports page during the week. List each team on one of the activity cards. List 25 professional football teams on cards as well. Put the college teams in one hat and the pro teams in another hat. Draw one card from each hat at a time. The first imaginary game is the first pro team drawn from the hat against the first college team drawn from the hat. Record the game on the worksheet. Continue in this fashion until 12 games are recorded on the worksheet.

Be sure to have the Sunday sports page and the Monday sports page for this activity. The college scores will be listed in the Sunday sports page while the professional scores will be listed in the Monday edition. Beside each team, list the number of points that were scored over the weekend. For example, if Michigan had an imaginary game against the Giants, students would find the Michigan score in the Sunday paper and record the points. Then they would find the Giants' score in the Monday paper and record the points. Continue in this fashion until all the scores are recorded by the names of the teams.

After the scores have been recorded, discuss the results of the games. Count to see if the pros won more games than the college teams. You may wish to count the points and see which team averaged the most points during the week. For a variation, have students choose high school teams from your area and pit them against professional teams or college teams. Even try your own middle school or elementary teams against a professional team!

College Bowl Day

Give students a copy of the worksheet titled "College Bowl Day" on page 70 before they leave for their holiday break. Most of the games will take place on the first or second day in January before students come back to school. Offer students extra credit points if they return the completed worksheet to you after the break.

The college bowl games decide who the national champion will be for the season. It is important to keep track of the teams' ranks in the polls leading up to the national championship game. The game itself will rotate among major bowl games—the Orange Bowl, the Rose Bowl, the Sugar Bowl, and the Fiesta Bowl. Many times the national champion is not always clear-cut because there are no unbeaten teams or there is more than one unbeaten team at the end of the season. For this activity, each student will pick a national champion based on the results of the major bowl games. Each student must then justify his or her choice.

Top 25 Colleges vs. the Pros

College team	Points	Pro team	Points	Winner

College Bowl Day

Track the major college bowls over the holiday break to see how the national champion in college football is crowned. Then answer the questions below.

Team	Ranking	vs.	Team	Ranking
Rose Bowl				
_____	_____		_____	_____
Orange Bowl				
_____	_____		_____	_____
Sugar Bowl				
_____	_____		_____	_____
Fiesta Bowl				
_____	_____		_____	_____
Another Bowl game that may impact the race for national champs				
_____	_____		_____	_____

How many undefeated teams are there in the major bowl games? _____

Which bowl game will decide the national championship this year? _____

Is the championship game a match-up between an undefeated team and a team with one

loss?_____ If so, how many other teams have just one loss? _____

Can you think of a better match-up for the national championship game? _____

Justify your choice for your national championship game.

_____

_____

Sample Basketball Box Score

West 137, East 126

East	26	33	38	35	—	132
West	33	31	33	36	—	133

EASTERN CONFERENCE ALL-STARS

Player	Min.	FG	FT	Reb O-T	A	PF	ST	TO	PTS
Carter	28	8-11	0-0	2-4	2	0	2	2	16
Hill	19	4-7	1-1	0-3	5	0	1	3	9
Mourning	27	7-11	1-2	2-7	1	4	3	1	15
Iverson	28	10-18	4-5	2-2	4	0	2	5	26
Jones	21	4-7	0-0	1-4	7	1	1	1	10
Houston	18	3-10	4-4	0-0	2	2	1	1	11
Davis	14	2-3	0-0	3-8	1	0	0	0	4
Miller	21	1-7	2-2	0-2	3	1	1	1	5
Mutombo	16	2-4	0-0	2-8	0	0	0	2	4
Robinson	17	5-10	0-0	2-6	0	0	0	0	10
Allen	17	4-13	5-6	1-1	2	2	3	3	14
Stackhouse	14	4-7	0-0	0-1	2	2	0	1	8
Totals	240	51-108	17-20	15-46	30	11	14	20	126

Team Rebounds: 8   **FG:** 47%   **FT:** 85%

WESTERN CONFERENCE ALL-STARS

Player	Min.	FG	FT	Reb O-T	A	PF	ST	TO	PTS
Garnett	35	10-19	4-4	3-10	5	1	1	0	24
Duncan	33	10-14	0-0	7-14	4	3	1	2	20
O'Neal	25	11-20	0-2	4-9	3	2	0	4	22
Bryant	28	7-16	0-0	1-1	3	3	2	1	15
Kidd	34	4-9	0-0	0-5	14	0	4	6	11
Payton	20	1-8	3-3	0-4	8	1	2	2	5
Stockton	11	5-5	0-0	0-0	2	2	1	0	10
Malone	3	0-1	0-0	0-0	0	0	0	0	0
Robinson	7	0-1	0-0	1-2	0	1	0	1	0
Wallace	21	3-6	3-4	2-4	0	0	1	0	9
Finley	10	5-6	0-0	0-1	0	0	0	1	11
Webber	13	3-10	0-0	3-8	3	2	1	2	6
Totals	240	61-115	10-13	21-58	42	15	13	19	137

Team Rebounds: 5   **FG:** 53%   **FT:** 77%

Blocked Shots: East—Mourning 4, Allen 1. West—O'Neal 3, Duncan 1, Garnett 1, Wallace 1.

3-Pt. Field Goals: East—7-23 (30%): Carter 0-2, Hill 0-1, Iverson 2-2, Jones 2-3, Houston 1-3, Miller 1-6, Allen 1-6. West—5-17 (29%): Garnett 0-1, Bryant 1-4, Kidd 3-6, Payton 0-4, Finley 1-2.

Technicals: None

A—18,325. T—2:12.

Basketball Scavenger Hunt #1

Find the following from the sports page and glue them on your answer sheet.

1. the name of a basketball player
2. the number of points a basketball player scored
3. a picture of a basketball
4. the name of a basketball team in your state
5. a basketball game that will be on TV
6. a player who stole the ball
7. a basketball team that is named for an animal
8. the name of a women's basketball team
9. a team that scored more than 50 points
10. the word *scored*

Basketball Scavenger Hunt #2

Find the following from the sports page and glue them on your answer sheet.

1. a city where an NBA game was played
2. a team that lost by fewer than 10 points
3. the word *foul*
4. a player who made a three-point field goal
5. a picture of a basketball player
6. a box score from any basketball game
7. city or state name of a college basketball team
8. a team that scored more than 70 points
9. a player who fouled out of a game
10. a team that is not named for an animal

Basketball Scavenger Hunt #3

Find the following from the sports page and glue them on your answer sheet.

1. a player who scored more than 15 points

2. a team that scored more than 25 points in the second quarter of a game

3. a game that had a total score of more than 150 points by both teams

4. a picture of a numbered basketball jersey

5. a team that lost a game that they were leading at halftime

6. the word *rim*

7. a game that went into overtime

8. a team that made at least five free throws

9. a player who had two or more assists

10. a female basketball player who scored more than 10 points

Basketball Scavenger Hunt #4

Find the following from the sports page and glue them on your answer sheet.

1. a team from the WNBA

2. a team that lost by more than 15 points

3. the word *defense*

4. a team that scored in single digits for one quarter of a basketball game

5. a high school or junior high school basketball team

6. a picture of a basketball player who is not in the NBA

7. a top-20 college team

8. a player who had two or more steals

9. a player who led his or her team in scoring

10. a game that had more than 100 points scored in the first half

Basketball Scavenger Hunt #5

Find the following from the sports page and glue them on your answer sheet.

1. a basketball team in first place in their conference or division

2. a player who made only one field goal in a basketball game

3. the word *guard*

4. a hyphenated word from a basketball article

5. a picture with at least one player from each team

6. a basketball player's last name that ends with an **n** or a **d**

7. a verb from a basketball headline

8. a ranked high school basketball team

9. a basketball game score with all odd numbers

10. a team that made more than half of their shots from the floor

Basketball Scavenger Hunt #6

Find the following from the sports page and glue them on your answer sheet.

1. a final basketball score with a zero in it

2. a female college basketball player

3. any player who made over 80 percent of his or her free throws

4. a picture of the lettering on a basketball

5. a basketball team that shot less than 50 percent for a game

6. a basketball team that scored double digits in all four quarters

7. a player who averages more than 10 points per game

8. the word *turnover*

9. a basketball team that made more than 50 percent of their shots

10. two basketball players who scored the same number of points

Basketball Scavenger Hunt #7

Find the following from the sports page and glue them on your answer sheet.

1. a non-professional team that scored in triple digits

2. a picture of a player's arms above his or her head

3. the name of a basketball coach

4. the nickname of a basketball player

5. a WNBA player who scored more than 20 points

6. a top-25 college team that lost

7. a basketball player who has three or more vowels in his or her last name

8. a letter designating a high school basketball class

9. the word *gym* or *gymnasium*

10. an apostrophe in a word from a basketball article

Basketball Scavenger Hunt #8

Find the following from the sports page and glue them on your answer sheet.

1. a player who blocked at least three shots

2. any basketball schedule

3. a center who scored at least 20 points

4. an adjective from a basketball headline

5. a player that took fewer than five shots during a game

6. a team that had more than one player foul out of the game

7. a picture of a player with an **s** on his or her jersey

8. the word *forward*

9. a common noun from a basketball article

10. a player who did not start in a game

Basketball Scavenger Hunt #9

Find the following from the sports page and glue them on your answer sheet.

1. a team that scored more points in the first quarter than in the fourth quarter

2. the time that a basketball game starts

3. the word *pass*

4. a quote from any basketball player

5. a simile from a basketball article

6. a game where both teams totaled 30 or more fouls

7. a picture that has a rim or a net in it

8. a player who had both double-digit assists and points

9. a team that had more than 30 rebounds

10. a player's assist total that is a factor of 30

Basketball Scavenger Hunt #10

Find the following from the sports page and glue them on your answer sheet.

1. an ordinal number from a basketball article

2. a team whose total score is a multiple of two numbers

3. a picture of a player slam dunking a basketball

4. a picture with four or more hands in it

5. a team that shot less than 40 percent for a game

6. the word *zone*

7. a player who made all of his or her free-throw attempts

8. a basketball player whose first or last name is a palindrome

9. onomatopoeia used in a basketball article

10. a team whose name is singular

Basketball Fun

Beginner

Use the worksheet titled "Basketball Fun (Beginner)" on page 78 for this activity. Also use the draft as explained in the introduction to determine selection order. Use this activity on a Monday during the NBA basketball season. You may wish to use this activity during the WNBA season as well. NBA and WNBA games are played during the week and on weekends. Students should be able to find statistics for their teams or players within a two- or three-day period.

After the draft, have students each choose a player from a professional team. Use the box scores from a previous day to help students make selections. The students will choose one player at a time. All participating students will choose player number one before they choose their next player. Then have students choose another player. You may wish to go in reverse draft order for the second round. For example, the last student to choose his or her player will be the first student to choose in the second round. Continue this process until each student has his or her five players and a substitute player. Students will write their players in the spaces given on the worksheet.

The next day in class, have students look at the sports page to find statistics for their players in the box score section. If a team did not play the night before, you may have to wait for the next game that the team plays to find statistics. After all students have completed the required information on the worksheets, total the scores and find the winner. The player with the most points will win the game.

Basketball Fun

Expert

Use the worksheet titled "Basketball Fun (Expert)" on page 79 for this activity. First, students will choose their players by position. They will each have two guards, two forwards, and a center as their starting lineups. They may use NBA players or WNBA players. However, if they choose someone to play guard for their imaginary team, that player must actually play that position in the pros. (If you are unsure of the positions of certain players, most sports sites on the Internet have profiles of every player in the NBA/WNBA.) Students will get the actual points their players score as well as bonus points for other statistical areas. Their teams will play against an imaginary team that always scores 100 points.

Have students select the teams of their choice, making sure that their players' positions actually match players in the NBA or WNBA. Record the names in the spaces provided on the worksheet. Have the sports page ready the next day in class. Students will go to the box scores to find the required information. If one of the teams did not play the night before, wait until the next time they play and use that box score.

Write in how many points each of the players scored. This is the base score for the team. Write it in the area provided. Then have students go to the bottom of the worksheet and write in the necessary statistical information. Students will receive points or have points deducted, depending on player performance. Add points received to the base points and deduct the other points. If the final point total is greater than 100, you are the winner!

Basketball Fun

Beginner

Choose your five players and a substitute after you have been given your picking order determined by the draft.

	Name	Team	Points
Player 1			
Player 2			
Player 3			
Player 4			
Player 5			
Player 6 (substitute)			

Total Points _____

Compare your total points with those of the other participants in the room to see who scored the most points.

Basketball Fun

Expert

Position	Player	Team	Points
Guard 1			
Guard 2			
Forward 1			
Forward 2			
Center			

Base points = total score of five players_____

❑ For each of your players who shot at least 50% from the field, add two points to the base score.

❑ For each three-point field goal that one of your players made, add an additional point.

❑ For each of your players who grabbed over seven rebounds, add one point.

❑ For each of your players who had over five assists, add one point.

❑ For each of your players who had more than three steals, add one point.

Total added to your base points _____

❑ For each time one of your players was assessed a technical foul, deduct two points.

❑ For each time one of your players fouled out, deduct two points.

Total number of points deducted _____

Your opponent's score is always 100. Adjust your base score by adding or deducting points and write your score on the scoreboard as the home team.

Home Team	Visiting Team
	100

NBA Basketball Name Fun

Find in the sports page names of professional basketball teams that fit the descriptions below. Cut and glue your answers in the spaces provided.

1. Get out of the kitchen if you can't stand this team. _____

2. You need this team to shoot yourself into space. _____

3. This team is faster than the speed of sound. _____

4. This team will cut your fingernails. _____

5. This team's members have stingers. _____

6. This team travels in packs. _____

7. Roll out the red carpet for this team. _____

8. This team is always in tune. _____

9. This team went with Lewis and Clark. _____

10. This team can blind you. _____

11. This team's members are worth their weight in gold. _____

12. A ball goes through this team. _____

13. Every year, this team runs through the streets of Spain. _____

Teacher Note: Fold answers under before photocopying this page for students.

Answers

1. Heat 2. Rockets 3. Supersonics 4. Clippers 5. Hornets 6. Timberwolves 7. Kings 8. Jazz 9. Trail Blazers 10. Suns 11. Nuggets 12. Nets 13. Bulls

(W)NBA Finals Fun

Pre-series

Use the sports page the week before the finals to find answers to the following questions about the two teams competing for the NBA championship.

1. Who led the Western Conference Champions in scoring for the season? How many points per game? _____

_____

2. Which team scored more points per game during the regular season?

_____

3. Which players led each of their teams in assists? How many assists did each player have? _____

_____

_____

4. What is the name of the arena or stadium at which the first game will take place? _____ What is the capacity? _____

5. Name the teams that each of the finalists beat to get to the series. _____

_____

_____

6. Which team had the best record during the regular season?

_____

7. Which team allowed the fewest points per game during the regular season?

_____

8. Name the coach of the Western Conference Champions. _____

9. Which starting lineup is the tallest? _____

10. Which player from either team averaged the most steals during the season?

_____

11. Who led the Eastern Conference Champions in rebounds? _____

12. Which center averaged the most points per game? _____

13. Which town will host four games, if necessary? _____

14. Which television network will cover the game? _____

15. Which team is at home first? _____

(W)NBA Finals Fun (cont.)

Predictions

Fill out this activity sheet before the final series begins. Use the sports page for ideas. Keep this sheet with you as you watch the series. Do not change answers once the series begins. Count points in parentheses for correct answers and total at the bottom of the page.

1. Name the player who will make the first three-point play. _____ (5)

2. Name the team that will take a time-out first. _____ (3)

3. Which team will score over 100 points in one game first? _____ (3)

4. Name the first team to win on the road in the series. _____ (3)

5. How many players will score more than 15 points in Game 2? _____ (5)

6. How many players will foul out of Game 4? _____ (5)

7. Which player will score the most points in Game 1? _____ (5)

8. Which player will be the leading rebounder for the series? _____ (5)

9. How many games in the series will the losing team win? _____ (5)

10. Which team will receive the first technical foul? _____ (3)

11. Which player will make the first free throw in Game 3. _____ (5)

12. Name the winner of the series. _____ (7)

Total Points _____

(W)NBA Finals Fun *(cont.)*

Post-series

Use the sports page the day after the (W)NBA Championship Series is over to help answer the following questions.

1. Who was the leading scorer for the series? _____

2. Did the champions win on their home court? _____

3. How many people attended the final game? _____

4. Which player was named as Most Valuable Player? _____

5. Which defense yielded the fewest points for the series? _____

   Was this also the winning team? _____

6. How many points did the champions average per game? _____

7. What was the average point differential for the series? _____

8. How many overtime games did the series produce? _____

9. Were any finals records set during the series? _____

   If so, name one. _____

10. How many fouls did each team get assessed during the series? _____

11. Who made the most three-point shots during the series? _____

12. Which team had the best shooting percentage for the series?

    _____

13. Which team shot the most free throws for the series? _____

14. How many total points were scored in the series? _____

15. How many time-outs were taken in the final game? _____

Basketball Scoring Pie Graphs

This activity is used for any basketball game that has the box score printed on the sports page. The pie graphs will be neater and easier to read if you find a game where there are six or seven scorers on the team. Each student will need a compass, a protractor, a ruler, and a copy of the worksheet "Basketball Scoring" on page 85.

Find any appropriate box score in the paper. On the worksheet, have students list all the players who scored. Write the team's total points in the space provided. Begin by making fractions for each player's point total. The numerator will be the points that the individual player scored. The denominator will be the total points for the team. Write the fractions in the space provided. Next, change the fractions to decimals by dividing the numerators by the denominators. Change the decimal to a percent by moving the decimal point two places to the right and rounding to the nearest whole number. This is the percentage of points that the player scored on the team. Record the information in the spaces provided on the worksheet.

Next, find out how much of the circle graph each player will fill. Write the players' percentages of scoring figures in the second table on the worksheet. In the next column, change the percent back to a decimal. For example, if a player accounted for 23% of his or her team's offense, you would change the percent to 0.23. Multiply the decimal of each player times 360, since there are 360 degrees in a circle. Round this number to the nearest whole number and write it in the column labeled "Degrees." This number represents the number of degrees on the pie graph that a player's score will fill. It will also represent the percentage of the team's points scored.

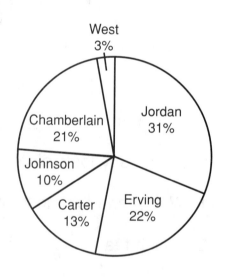

Now, hand each student a piece of white 8" x 12" (20 cm x 30 cm) construction paper. Have the students use their compasses to draw the largest circle possible on the paper. Use a pencil to make the point in the middle visible. Then draw a line to the edge of a circle to make a radius. Use the information on the table on the bottom of the worksheet and a protractor to draw the rest of the lines. For example, a player scoring 23% of his or her team's points would account for an 83-degree section of the circle. Place the sight of the protractor on the center point and align the leading edge with the radius. Mark the number for 83 degrees and connect a line from the center of the circle to the mark at 83 degrees. Shade the pie shape any color. Remember that this shape covers 23% of the circle. It is easier for students to think that they have covered 23% instead of 83 degrees.

Continue in this manner until all of the scorers have been added to the pie graph. Students can check their calculations by adding all their degrees and percentage figures. The degree figures should add up to 360. The percentage figures should add up to 100. Have students label their graphs with appropriate titles at the top. Color all the pie shapes in different colors and label each section with a player's name. For fun, have students graph one of their own basketball games!

84

Basketball Scoring: Pie Graphs

Student Name _____

Team Name and Points Scored_____

Player	Points Scored	Fraction	Percentage	Decimal

Player	Percentage of Points Scored	Decimal	Degrees

NBA All-Stars

Each year in February, the NBA holds its annual All-Star game. The teams are comprised of players from the two divisions in the NBA: the Eastern Conference and the Western Conference. These players are selected by fans who vote for players of their choice throughout the year. In this activity, students will create their own All-Star teams and compare them to the real All-Star team. Each participating student will need a copy of the worksheet "NBA All-Stars" on page 87.

Pass out the worksheets during the first week of December. Inform students that they will make an All-Star team. They will list actual NBA players by their positions. For each conference they will have a starting lineup and a second-team lineup. Set a due date for this activity for the first week in January after students return from winter holiday break. Students may use the sports page to help make selections. Instruct students to look at the box scores to see which players score the most points and at the statistics to find the leaders in steals, rebounding, and assists.

Have the students fill out the worksheet during their spare time. You may wish to devise a point system and hold an All-Star competition. For example, for every player whom students name to the first team correctly, they will be awarded five points. For each player whom students name to the second team correctly, they will be awarded two points. If a student lists a player who is not on the exact team, he or she will be awarded one point.

Look for information about the All-Star game in the sports page. The final selections will be announced about two weeks before the game. Students will be able to check their worksheets at this time.

My All-Stars

Guard: Michael Jordan

Guard: Magic Johnson

Forward: Julius Erving

Forward: Vince Carter

Center: Wilt Chamberlain

Basketball Centers

This activity will help students understand just how tall professional or college basketball players really are! Each participating student will need a copy of the activity sheet titled "Basketball Centers." Have each student find the heights of three professional or collegiate basketball centers. This should be accomplished at the beginning of the basketball season (in the fall) when newspapers print player rosters. Another fun way to find players' heights is to access a team's Web site. All professional teams have a site on the Internet that includes player information.

Give each student a copy of the activity sheet on page 88. The sheet is actually a scale. The numbers on the left represent height in feet and inches. Have students draw lines on the scale that represent their players in feet and inches. Then measure each participating student, and have him or her draw a line on the scale. Allow students to have fun making stick figures out of the lines they have drawn. Put jerseys on the figures and color them. Students can also figure out how many times taller a center is than they are. Find the ratio of the scale by measuring the line and writing it in ratio form as in this example: 80:5 or reduce to 16:1.

NBA All-Stars

Eastern Conference Predictions

First Team	Second Team
Guard _____	Guard _____
Guard _____	Guard _____
Forward_____	Forward_____
Forward_____	Forward_____
Center_____	Center_____

Western Conference Predictions

First Team	Second Team
Guard _____	Guard _____
Guard _____	Guard _____
Forward_____	Forward_____
Forward_____	Forward_____
Center_____	Center_____

Choose the player that you think will be named MVP. _____

How many points do you think both teams will score? _____

Basketball Centers

Student Name _____

Name three centers and list their heights in feet and inches (for example, 7' 3").

Centers	Height

8'	•
7' 6"	•
7'	•
6' 6"	•
6'	•
5' 6"	•
5'	•
4' 6"	•
4'	•
3' 6"	•
3'	•
2' 6"	•
2'	•
1' 6"	•
1'	•
0' 6"	•

0' 0" _____

List the four people (the three centers and yourself) in order from tallest to shortest.

_____ _____ _____ _____

March Madness

Each year in March, the NCAA holds the annual Division 1 NCAA Basketball Championship. The field consists of the top 64 teams in the country as selected by a special committee. The tournament decides the college basketball national champion. The committee releases the names of the entrants on a Sunday afternoon before the tournament. The sports page will have a copy of the tournament bracket the following Monday.

Cut the bracket from the sports page and make copies for each participating student. You may wish to enlarge it so that the bracket takes the entire page. Have students write the teams that they think will win the first-round games into the spaces provided on the bracket. This will automatically line up the second-round games. There will be 32 teams left in the tournament at this point. Then have students write their second-round choices in the spaces on the bracket. Continue this until the participants have chosen the two teams that they feel will compete for the national championship. Then write the team that they think will win the game in the center of the bracket. There are six rounds, including the championship game.

March						
			1	2	3	4
5	6	7	8	9	10	11
12	13	14	15	16	17	18
19	20	21	22	23	24	25
26	27	28	29	30	31	

Devise a point value for each round. For example, for each first-round game picked correctly, students will gain one point. For each second-round game chosen correctly, students will get two points. Continue this point format until you get to the final four. Make the last three games of the tournament worth more points. Have students circle their winners as the tournament progresses. Students can keep track of their own points. Be sure to collect all the entries from participants before Thursday of tournament week. The first games usually begin on Thursday morning. You may wish to photocopy each student's bracket after completion and hand back the originals so that they are not tempted to change teams after the tournament begins.

Bingo Basketball Scores

Use this activity when you have multiple copies of a newspaper for class members during basketball season. Saturday's edition of the sports page will work well because it will have many scores published. Divide the class into groups of 4–5 students. Give each group a copy of the worksheet "Bingo Basketball Scores" on page 90.

When the teacher says "Go!" students will go through the sports page and find teams' final scores that match the numbers on the grid. The scores can be from professional, college, high school, or any other game that is published. Then have students cut out the name of that team and glue it on the grid over that number. The first group that gets three scores in a row will yell "Bingo!" The scores may run horizontally, vertically, or diagonally. The boxes that say "free" in them allow students to leave that space open. If students find three in a row too easy, ask them to find five in a row the next time you play the game. Check the groups' results with your sports page upon completion.

Bingo Basketball Scores

110	56	113	98	86	FREE	57	64	103	83
121	73	65	51	105	68	53	84	85	78
50	44	91	69	82	108	65	71	43	38
76	80	93	48	123	106	44	77	59	54
36	52	110	111	45	FREE	88	97	61	76
29	112	89	42	55	120	104	62	43	85
75	67	83	89	95	98	109	110	61	34
54	71	45	56	76	80	74	33	48	87
99	91	111	119	63	57	68	73	92	110
FREE	29	79	82	113	105	96	81	66	70

Top 25 College Basketball Teams

This activity will work equally well with the men's top 25 college basketball poll and the women's top 25 basketball poll. Divide the class into groups and give each group a copy of the outline map of the United States on page 92. Also give each group a copy of a sports page with the top 25 men's or women's basketball poll. These are usually published on Mondays or Tuesdays during the college basketball season. Each group will also need access to reference materials such as sports almanacs, encyclopedias, and atlases. Students may also wish to use the Internet for research.

Students will find the locations of the top 25 college basketball teams and draw dots on the map to represent their locations. To accomplish this, students should first locate the city where the college or university is, then refer to a map or atlas before plotting the point. After the location is found and students plot the point, have them write the corresponding poll number by that point. For example, if the University of Kentucky is the #1 ranked team, students would write the number "1" by the point at Lexington.

After students finish the maps, have them answer the questions at the bottom of the page. Lead the class in a discussion about the locations of the top 25 college basketball teams.

Basketball Dream Team

In this activity, students will choose players from different levels and see how many points their dream team can score. You will need to give each class member a copy of the worksheet titled "Basketball Dream Team" on page 93. Students will need access to sports pages on a daily basis during this activity.

Have students each choose their dream team and record it on the worksheet in the spaces provided. Each student must choose a player from each of the following basketball teams: a local high school girls' team, a local high school boys' team, a women's college team, a men's college team, and an NBA team. Have students work independently so that everyone does not use the same players. Then have students make their schedule of the games they wish to play. Each student must choose for their dream team's opponents one high school girl's team, one high school boys team, a college women's team, a college men's team, and an NBA team.

Students will need to read the sports page to find out how many points each of his or her players score in their next game. This may require the teacher to save the sports page from the weekend editions to bring to class on Monday. Students may also access the Internet to find both local and national scores from most games. Students will also need to record the number of points their opponents score in their next game. Fill in the players' scores and the scores of the opponents. Then have students total the records of their dream teams to see how they fared.

Outline Map of the United States

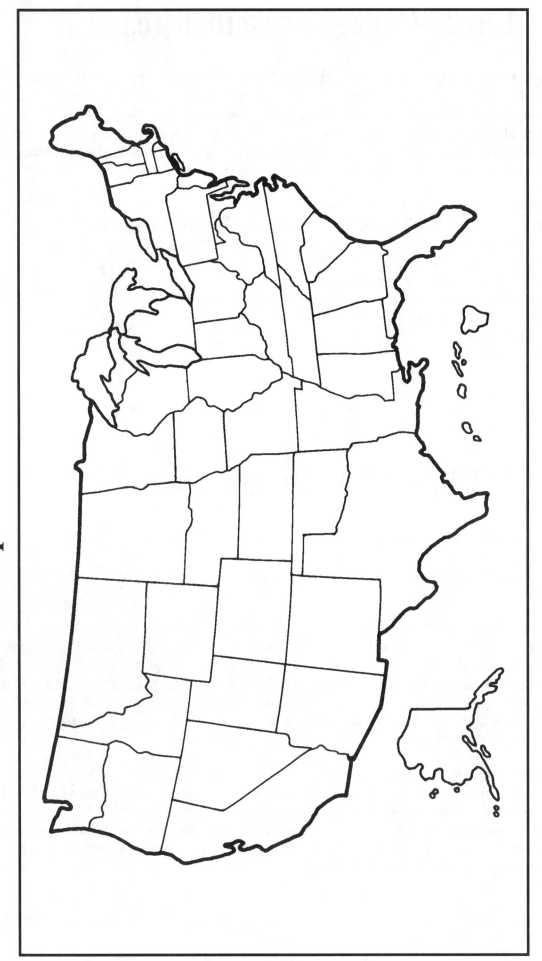

Where do most of the top 25 teams seem to be on the map? _____

Hypothesize: Explain the distribution of the top 25 college basketball teams.

Basketball Dream Team

Find players from each category to make your dream team.

Category	Player	Team	Points Scored in Next Game
High School Boys' Team			
High School Girls' Team			
Women's College Team			
Men's College Team			
NBA Team			

Total the number of points scored by your dream team._____

Make your schedule by choosing a team in each category.

Category	Opponent (Team)	Opponent's Score from their Next Game	Dream Team's Score from Above
High School Boys' Team			
High School Girls' Team			
Women's College Team			
Men's College Team			
NBA Team			

What is the win/loss record of your dream team?_____

Sample Hockey Box Score

Anaheim 4, Dallas 2

	1st	2nd	3rd		TOTAL
Anaheim	0	2	2	—	4
Dallas	2	0	0	—	2

FIRST PERIOD Scoring: 1. Dallas, Hull 8 (Keane, Matvichuk), 3:15. 2. Dallas, Sim 3 (Skrudland, Murray), 7:12. Penalties: J Marshall, Ana (double roughing minor), 17:57; Wright, Dal (double roughing minor), 17:57.

SECOND PERIOD Scoring: 3. Anaheim, Hrkac 1 (Grimson, J. Nielsen), 11:35. 4. Anaheim, Selanne 9 (unassisted), 16:51. Penalties: Havelid, Ana (interference), 1:40; Jackman, Dal (tripping), 18:05.

THIRD PERIOD Scoring: 5. Anaheim, Selanne 10 (Rucchin, P. Kariya), 9:27. 6. Anaheim, P. Kariya 16 (unassisted—empty net), 19:16. Penalties: J. Marshall, Ana (roughing), 4:29.

Shots on goal:

	1st	2nd	3rd		TOTAL
Anaheim	9	9	5	—	23
Dallas	4	5	10	—	19

Power Play Conversions: Ana 0 of 3, Dal 0 of 3. Goalies: Anaheim, G. Hebert (19 shots, 17 saves; record 9–10–1). Dallas, Belfour (23 shots, 19 saves; record 8–8–2). A: 17,001.

Individual Player Statistics

Anaheim

	G	A	+/-	Shots
Aalto	0	0	even	2
Cullen	0	0	even	0
Donato	0	0	even	0
Grimson	0	1	even	0
Havelid	0	0	+1	3
Hrkac	1	0	even	1
J. Nielsen	0	1	even	2
J. Marshall	0	0	+1	0
Kohn	0	0	even	1
Leclerc	0	0	even	1
McInnis	0	0	even	1
Olausson	0	0	+1	1
P. Kariya	1	1	+2	2
Rucchin	0	1	+2	1
Salei	0	0	+3	2
Selanne	2	0	+2	4
Tmka	0	0	-1	1
Tverdovsky	0	0	-1	1

Dallas

	G	A	+/-	Shots
Carbonneau	0	0	even	1
Hatcher	0	0	-2	1
Hull	1	0	-2	3
Jackman	0	0	even	0
Keane	0	1	-1	0
Langenbrunner	0	0	even	1
Lukowich	0	0	even	1
Matvichuk	0	1	-1	0
Modano	0	0	-2	1
Morrow	0	0	even	1
Murray	0	0	even	1
Nieuwendyk	0	0	-1	1
Sim	1	0	even	4
Skrudland	0	1	even	1
Sloan	0	0	even	0
Sydor	0	0	-2	1
Wright	0	0	even	0
Zubov	0	0	even	2

Hockey Scavenger Hunts #1

Find the following from the sports page and glue them on your answer sheet.

1. the word *goal*

2. the name of any hockey team

3. a hockey player who scored a goal

4. a city where an NHL team plays

5. a picture of a hockey player

6. a game where more than three goals were scored

7. a hockey headline

8. a team that won a hockey game

9. a noun from a hockey article

10. the number of periods in a hockey game

Hockey Scavenger Hunts #2

Find the following from the sports page and glue them on your answer sheet.

1. a hockey team that is not named for an animal

2. a game that's total goals were an even number.

3. a player who had three or more points

4. a verb from a hockey headline

5. a picture that has ice in it

6. a quote from a hockey player

7. the word *tie*

8. a team that lost by more than one goal

9. a game that went to overtime

10. the line score from a hockey game

Hockey Scavenger Hunts #3

Find the following from the sports page and glue them on your answer sheet.

1. a picture of a hockey player wearing a white jersey

2. the name of a defenseman from any hockey team

3. a game where each team scored at least two goals

4. an adjective that describes a hockey team

5. the word *penalty*

6. a team that plays in Canada

7. a game where each team scored odd numbers

8. the logo of any NHL hockey team

9. a game attended by more than 12,000 people

10. a player who gave up a goal

Hockey Scavenger Hunts #4

Find the following from the sports page and glue them on your answer sheet.

1. the name of a player that ends in **g**

2. a team with a winning record

3. the word *net*

4. the name of a college or high school hockey team

5. a game that ended with a total score that is a multiple of three

6. a team that lost on their home ice

7. a picture with a hockey stick in it

8. an international hockey game

9. a player who led his team in points

10. a player who had the game-winning goal

Hockey Scavenger Hunts #5

Find the following from the sports page and glue them on your answer sheet.

1. a team that did not score any goals

2. a picture of a number on a jersey

3. a player who had the number of points that is a multiple of 4

4. a game's total score that is a factor of 25

5. a team with more losses than ties or wins

6. a game that was played at night

7. a team that is leading its division

8. the word *period*

9. a conjunction from a hockey article

10. a player who was in the penalty box

Hockey Scavenger Hunts #6

Find the following from the sports page and glue them on your answer sheet.

1. a team that lost a game that it was leading

2. a team that scored one goal in the first period

3. the word *puck*

4. a hockey team that is named for a predator of the sea

5. a game played by two Canadian teams

6. a simile from a hockey article

7. a game that was televised

8. a picture that has a hockey net in it

9. name of a hockey player who has the same number of letters in his first and last names

10. a final score that includes a square number

Hockey Fun

Beginner

Each participating student will be assigned an NHL Hockey team. Give each student copies of the worksheets titled "Activity Cards" and "Hockey Fun (Beginner)." Each student will also need a box score from a hockey game with his or her team in it.

Have each student write his or her hockey players on separate activity cards; be sure not to include goalies. Have students each pick seven players of their choice from the box score and list them on the "Hockey Fun (Beginner)" worksheet in any order. After students finish putting players' names on cards, have all students put their cards into the hat or other container. While students are putting names on their activity cards, the teacher will fill out cards, too. Write the word *steal* on one card. Write the word *miss* on another card. Write the word *save* on two separate cards, and write the word *goal* on another card. The teacher will then put his or her cards in a separate "hat" or container for drawing.

The teacher will draw a player name out of the first hat and then will read the name aloud to the class. Have the student who has the player raise his or her hand. Then draw a card out of the other hat. The word *miss* will mean that the player missed his attempt at goal. The word *steal* will mean that the puck was stolen. The word *save* will mean that the goalie saved the shot from going into the net. The word *goal* will mean that the player scored a goal. For every draw that the teacher makes from the hat, the student will have a 25% chance of his or her player scoring a goal. Students will keep track of their players' performances by putting checkmarks in the appropriate boxes on their worksheets.

After all the names have been drawn, students will calculate their goals and write the totals at the bottom of the worksheets in the space provided. If time constraints are necessary, inform students that the drawings will take place for only a given number of minutes. The student with the most goals at the end of the game wins.

Expert

Give each participating student a copy of the "Hockey Fun (Expert)" worksheet on page 100. Students will assemble imaginary hockey teams and compete against their classmates.

Hold the draft as explained in the introduction to determine the order in which students will choose players. Students will choose five players (excluding goalies) for their hockey teams. After the worksheets have been filled in with the students' players, use the sports page for the following 2–3 days until all the statistical information has been completed. This may take a few days because teams do not play a game every night during the regular season. Make sure that students use the information from the next game for each of their players. Also, be sure to have students list their opponents in the space provided. The opponent is the team in the box scores that they must beat. For example, if the student picked the Rangers as his or her opponent, the Rangers' score in their next game is the score he or she will have to beat.

After students collect information from the box scores, total the results in the space provided on the worksheet. Have students check the scores of their opponents and write them in the spaces provided. If the students' imaginary teams are able to score more goals than their opponents, they win the games. Also check to see which student has the best score in the class. Students will calculate statistics for points at the bottom of the worksheets.

Hockey Fun

Beginner

As your teacher calls the names of your players, listen carefully to see if they scored a goal, missed the shot, had the puck stolen, or the goalie saved the shot. Place an **X** in the appropriate box for each player.

Player Name	Team	Goal	Miss	Steal	Save

Write the total number of goals here. _____

Hockey Fun

Expert

Player	Team	Goals	Assists

Name of the team you wish to play against_____

Total goals of your five players after each ones next game_____

Total score of your opponent after their next game_____

Challenge: In hockey, points track player performance. A player receives points for making goals and assists. Goals and assists are each worth one point. Calculate how many points each of your players made in the game for which you recorded information above.

NHL Hockey Name Fun

Find in the sports page professional hockey teams that fit the descriptions below. Cut and glue your answers in the spaces provided.

1. This team is never on the ground. _____

2. This team will burn you. _____

3. This team can bury you alive. _____

4. This team's members will fall from the trees.

   _____

5. This team's members are stars on the map.

   _____

6. This team's members might know the president.

   _____

7. You carry this team by your side. _____

8. This team loves dark clouds. _____

9. This team might be pink. _____

10. You can feel this team circling. _____

11. This team will hibernate. _____

12. You can see this team on clear nights. _____

13. This team's members wear crowns. _____

Teacher Note: Fold answers under before photocopying this page for students.

Answers

1. Flyers 2. Flames 3. Avalanche 4. Maple Leafs 5. Capitols 6. Senators 7. Sabres 8. Lightning 9. Panthers 10. Sharks 11. Bruins 12. Stars 13. Kings

Stanley Cup Fun

Pre-series

Look at the sports page the week before the Stanley Cup. Find answers to the following questions about the two teams competing for the cup.

1. Which team will host the first game of the series? _____

2. How many games did each team win during the regular season? _____

3. Which team had the most penalties during the playoffs? _____

4. How many games will be played in Canada? _____

5. Which player from each team had the most assists? _____

6. Name a player from each team who is injured. _____

   _____

7. Name the two arenas where the games will be played. _____

   _____

8. If the series lasts seven games and each game is a sellout, about how many spectators will watch the series in person? _____

9. Name the starting goalies from each team. _____

   _____

10. Which of the goalies gave up the fewest number of goals during the regular season? _____

11. Name the player from either side who had the most points during the regular season. _____

12. Which team had the most ties during the regular season? _____

13. Which player from either team scored the most goals during the regular season? _____

14. Which team played more games during the playoffs? _____

15. Which team is based farthest to the north? _____

Stanley Cup Fun *(cont.)*

Predictions

Complete this activity before the Stanley Cup begins. Have this sheet with you as you watch the series. Do not change any of your answers after the games begin. Point values for each question are listed in parentheses. Count the number of points you get throughout the series and write the total at the bottom.

1. Which player will score the first goal of the series. _____ (5)

2. Which team will win Game 3? _____ (3)

3. How many total goals will be scored in Game 2? _____ (5)

4. Name the player who will have the most points after the first two games. _____ (5)

5. How many games will the series last? _____ 3)

6. Name the goalie who will give up the fewest goals in the series.

   _____ (3)

7. Name the team that will score consecutive goals first.

   _____ (3)

8. Which player will get penalized first? _____ (5)

9. Which team will get called for icing first? _____ (3)

10. How many games will go to overtime in the series? _____ (3)

11. Which team will win the opening face-off? _____ (3)

12. Which team will win the Stanley Cup? _____ (7)

Total points _____

Stanley Cup Fun *(cont.)*

Post-series

Use the sports page the day after the Stanley Cup is over to help answer the following questions.

1. How many games did the series last? _____

2. Which player from each team had the most points? _____

    _____

3. Did the champions win on their own ice? _____

4. Which goalie allowed the fewest goals? _____

5. What was the attendance of the final game? _____

6. Which player from either team scored the most goals?

    _____

7. Which team had the most penalty time for the series? _____

8. Which player was named Most Valuable Player for the series?

    _____

9. Which game produced the most goals of the series?

    _____

10. Which game of the series produced the fewest goals?

    _____

11. What was the average number of goals scored for each game of the series? _____

12. Name a player who was injured in the series. _____

13. Name any NHL Stanley Cup Finals records that were broken during the series. _____

    _____

14. Did any of the games in this series go to overtime? _____ If so name one. _____

15. About how far did each visiting team have to travel to get to each home team's arena?

    _____

Hockey Scoring by Position

Use the worksheet on page 106 to see which players in hockey score the most goals. Students will track NHL games for a number of days, using the box scores on the sports page. Use all the games for that day. Make a tally mark under the position for each goal and each assist. For example, if a center on a team scored a goal, put a tally mark under the word "Center" on the worksheet. Continue in this manner until all the goals for all of the games that day are accounted for. (If you are unsure of the positions of certain players, most sports sites on the Internet have profiles of every player in the NHL.) Have students track goals for at least three days.

When students finish the top part of the worksheet, have them count the tally marks and total the goals and assists in the spaces provided. Use reference materials to find answers to the questions at the bottom of the worksheet. Allow students to use sports encyclopedias, almanacs, or the Internet to answer the questions.

NHL Attendance

Use the worksheet titled "NHL Attendance" on page 107 to find which hockey teams have the best fan support. The worksheet is set up like a bar graph. Students will choose a hockey team and follow attendance figures in the box scores from the sports page. Encourage participants to graph different teams. After each game, color the lines on the graph to measure attendance. Make sure that students use home game attendance figures for the team that they choose to follow. Graph each team's home games and see which team is able get to the end of the graph (1,000,000) first! Each increment on the bar graph represents 50,000 spectators. Write actual attendance numbers in the spaces to the right of the graph.

Hockey Scoring by Position

Place tally marks in the correct box for every goal scored and each assist registered.

Right Wing	Left Wing	Center	Goalie	Defensemen

Totals

_____   _____   _____   _____   _____

Use reference materials and the Internet to find out who some of the great scorers are in the history of the NHL. Write the names and positions of at least five in the spaces provided.

Leading NHL Scorers

_____   _____

_____   _____

_____

Which position did most of the all-time leading scorers play? _____

For which position above did you make the most tally marks? _____

Does your research seem to support the statistics you collected? _____

Explain _____

_____

_____

NHL Attendance

Team Name _____

NHL Attendance (in thousands)

	1	2	3	4	5	6	7	8	9	10
1,000										
950										
900										
850										
800										
750										
700										
650										
600										
550										
500										
450										
400										
350										
300										
250										
200										
150										
100										
50										
0										
Game	1	2	3	4	5	6	7	8	9	10

Professional Sports Salaries

Professional athletes use agents to request higher salaries based on player performance. The agents propose a salary figure on behalf of the player to the owner of the team. The owner and his or her staff will present an alternate figure to try to get the player to accept an offer. Usually, the two sides meet somewhere in the middle of these negotiations. Have students search the sports page to find instances where owners and players have salary disputes. Encourage students to find professional baseball, football, or basketball players. Find instances where professional athletes agreed to accept a salary. The salary figure will represent the monetary amount that the athlete will be paid over a given number of years in exchange for his or her athletic services. On the worksheet "Professional Sports Salaries" on page 109, have students record the information in the spaces provided for salaried players.

Students will figure out how much money a professional athlete makes per game. To accomplish this, determine how much money a contract will pay a player for each year. Divide the monetary figure by the number of years a contract is extended to. Then find how much the athlete will make in one game by dividing by the number of games. Have students do an independent research project to determine how much athletes from individual sports (e.g., tennis, golf, bowling, etc.) make. Find out how their incomes compare to those of athletes who compete in team sports.

Date _3-3-03_

Pay to: _J.R. Moore_ $ 4,700,000.00

Amount: _four million seven hundred thousand 0/100_ cents

For: _catching footballs_   Signature: _Theo Knerz_

Sports Page Venn Diagram

Find the worksheet titled "Sports Page Venn Diagram" on page 110 for this activity. Students will learn to find relationships between different groups of teams or players on the sports page. Give each student a copy of the worksheet and a sports page. Allow students to work in groups, if you desire.

Have students write lists of your choice in circles A and B. For example, write all the team names in the American League in circle A and all the team names in the National League in circle B. At this point do not allow students to write anything in the middle area where the circles intersect. Have students examine the lists carefully. Ask them to think of ways those teams in one circle might be related to teams in the other circle. Some examples might include teams named after animals or teams that have winning records. These teams will be listed in the area where the circles intersect. There are many possibilities for such an example. Accept reasonable responses.

Think of your own ways to use the Venn diagram. List random sports or events in the circles and allow students to synthesize results. List players from different sports or even sporting implements such as golf clubs, baseball bats, fishing poles, etc. Depending on the age group you teach, you may wish to put words in the circles yourself before you photocopy and distribute the diagram.

Professional Sports Salaries

Find articles where professional athletes are trying to increase the monetary value of their contracts. Follow the story in the sports page each day. Then figure out the terms of the contract and answer the questions below. Try to find one professional basketball player, one professional football player, and one professional baseball player.

Basketball

Name of player _____ Name of team _____

For how many years did the player sign? _____

How much money will the player make? _____

Salary per year: Total value of contract divided by number of years _____

Salary per game: Money per year divided by 82 (games in season) _____

Football

Name of player _____ Name of team _____

For how many years did the player sign? _____

How much money will the player make? _____

Salary per year: Total value of contract divided by number of years _____

Salary per game: Money per year divided by 16 (games in season) _____

Baseball

Name of player _____ Name of team _____

For how many years did the player sign? _____

How much money will the player make? _____

Salary per year: Total value of contract divided by number of years _____

Salary per game: Money per year divided by 162 (games in season) _____

Sports Page Venn Diagram

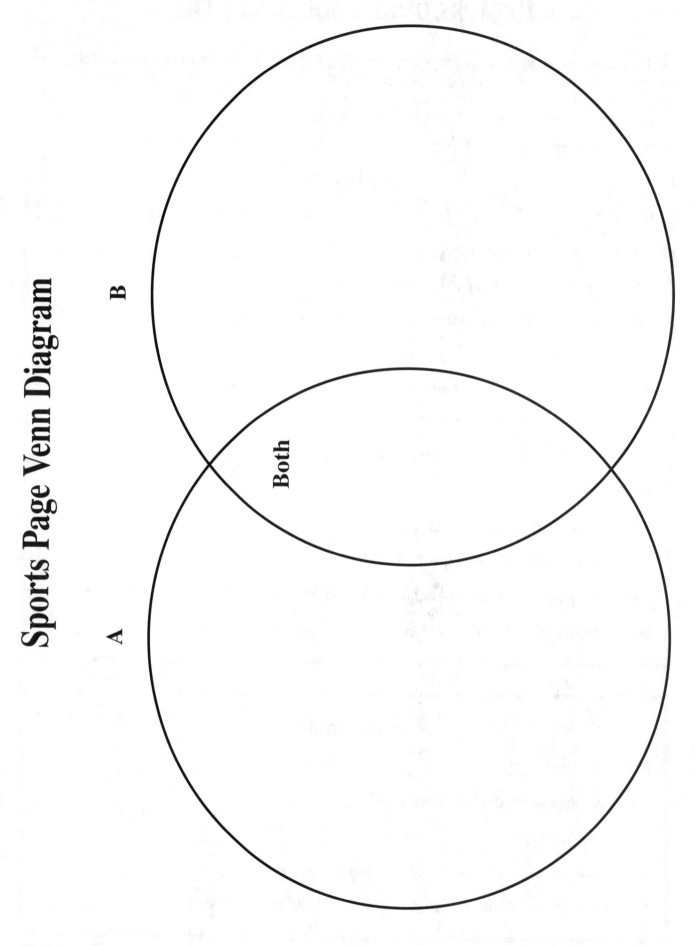

A

B

Both

Sports Page Scavenger Hunt #1

Find the following items from the sports page and glue them on your answer sheet.

1. a picture of an athlete

2. the word *sports*

3. a sport that uses a ball

4. a team that won

5. a sport not played in a stadium

6. a team that played away from home

7. any circle from the sports page

8. the name of a college

9. a coach's name

10. a team or player in the headlines

Sports Page Scavenger Hunt #2

Find the following items from the sports page and glue them on your answer sheet.

1. any logo

2. the word *versus* (or *vs.*)

3. a time that a game will be played

4. a picture of a player in uniform

5. a sport played indoors

6. an individual sport

7. an event that will be televised

8. an athlete with two syllables in his or her last name

9. a team that is named for an animal

10. a square number from the sports page

Sports Page Scavenger Hunt #3

Find the following items from the sports page and glue them on your answer sheet.

1. a noun from the sports page

2. the name of a conference or division

3. an advertisement from the sports page

4. any score that ends in even numbers

5. the word *game*

6. a picture of an athlete with a ball

7. an abbreviation

8. the name of a player that ends in **s**

9. any upcoming game or event

10. a high school sport

Sports Page Scavenger Hunt #4

Find the following items from the sports page and glue them on your answer sheet.

1. a verb from the headlines

2. a sport where a ball is kicked

3. a picture of an animal

4. a player who has double consonants in his or her name

5. the words *Associated Press* or *AP*

6. the record of a team

7. a game that featured two winning teams

8. a sport where the audience has to be quiet

9. a word with an apostrophe in it

10. an event played in your home state

Sports Page Scavenger Hunt #5

Find the following items from the sports page and glue them on your answer sheet.

1. the date of your sports page

2. the word for any color (example: blue)

3. a headline about any tournament

4. an event played by two contestants

5. a headline about a racing event

6. the word *Sunday*

7. a sport with four quarters

8. a total score that is divisible by three

9. any rectangle from the sports page

10. a person who caught a ball

Sports Page Scavenger Hunt #6

Find the following items from the sports page and glue them on your answer sheet.

1. a three-syllable team name

2. the name of a sportswriter

3. a city or town more than 100 miles from your school

4. a simile from the sports page

5. a picture of a coach or manager

6. a quote from a player or coach

7. a sport that is not timed

8. a team that doubled their opponent's score

9. how long an event took

10. a sport not played on grass

Sports Page Scavenger Hunt #7

Find the following items from the sports page and glue them on your answer sheet.

1. the word *defense*

2. a team ranked number 1 in a poll

3. any upset

4. a picture of an umpire or a referee

5. a distance from the sports page

6. a team or city with two words in its name

7. any polygon from the sports page

8. any contraction from the sports page

9. a player who has one syllable in both first and last names

10. a sport that doesn't use a ball

Sports Page Scavenger Hunt #8

Find the following items from the sports page and glue them on your answer sheet.

1. the word *rally*

2. an article that was continued

3. a hyphenated word from the sports page

4. any player who was injured

5. an adjective from a headline

6. a metaphor from the sports page

7. a logo of a professional sports league

8. a sport where no score is kept

9. a fraction or decimal from the sports page

10. a team that scored more than 10 points in the second quarter

Sports Page Scavenger Hunt #9

Find the following items from the sports page and glue them on your answer sheet.

1. a player who hit a ball

2. a team that is not an animal

3. the word *big*

4. a pronoun from the sports page

5. a sport that is always played outdoors

6. a headline that uses alliteration

7. the name of the newspaper that printed this sports page

8. an integer

9. a picture of a sports fan

10. a city or team name with four syllables

Sports Page Scavenger Hunt #10

Find the following items from the sports page and glue them on your answer sheet.

1. a professional team from California

2. a picture of any female athlete

3. an event attended by more than 12,000 people

4. a byline from the sports page

5. an event that happened north of your school

6. the name of a sports photographer

7. sum of the digits of a score that equals 10

8. an example of hyperbole

9. the word *effort*

10. a conjunction used in a article

Game Time Terms

Find in the sports page the name of a sport that matches each term or phrase. Cut it out and glue it in the space provided.

1. Fore! _____

2. dunk _____

3. dig _____

4. bullpen _____

5. deuce _____

6. spike _____

7. love _____

8. gridiron _____

9. icing _____

10. pole _____

11. down the stretch _____

12. header _____

13. Hail Mary _____

Teacher Note: Fold answers under before photocopying this page for students.

Answers:

1. Golf 2. Basketball 3. Volleyball 4. Baseball 5. Tennis 6. Volleyball 7. Tennis 8. Football
9. Hockey 10. Racecar driving 11. Horseracing 12. Soccer 13. Football

Volleyball Scavenger Hunt

Find the following volleyball items from the sports page and glue them on your answer sheet.

1. the word *match*
2. a game that lasted at least four sets
3. an article about a college volleyball team
4. a picture with a volleyball net in it
5. a team that had more than 20 kills
6. a player whose total number of digs was in the double digits
7. a game where both teams points totaled more than 27
8. the name of a high school volleyball player
9. a game where a team won every other set
10. a picture of a volleyball player with both of his or her feet off the ground

Soccer Scavenger Hunt

Find the following soccer items from the sports page and glue them to your answer sheet.

1. a female high-school soccer player
2. a soccer game where one team did not score
3. a player who had more than five saves
4. the word *goal*
5. a team that had more than 7 corner kicks
6. a professional soccer team
7. a picture of a soccer ball
8. a game total by both teams that is a factor of 20
9. the name of a goalkeeper
10. a team that doubled their opponent in shots

Sports Page Volleyball

This activity is designed for two players competing against each other. The players will need a coin or other round marker, a sports page, a pencil, and a piece of scratch paper. The game will follow volleyball rules.

One player will start as the server. The server will flip the coin in the air until it lands on the box-score section of the sports page. Without moving the coin, the server will trace an outline around the coin on the paper. The players will remove the coin and examine the area made by the outline of the coin. The digits in the area determine whether or not the server will gain a point. Find the largest single digit in the outline of the coin. If no digits are found in the outlined area, the player will serve until a digit is found. After the server has a digit, the other player will toss the coin on the paper and outline his or her position. This player will find the largest digit in his or her area. If this digit is larger than the digit of the server, the player gains service. If not, the server gets the point.

Continue the game in this manner, following the rules of volleyball. The student who has service to start the game will continue to serve until the opposing player has a higher digit on the coin toss. When the player not serving gets a higher digit, he or she will get to serve, but will not receive a point—as in volleyball, a player can only win a point when he or she is serving. The first player to get to 15 points will win the game. The player must win by two points or the game will continue. Volleyball is played in sets. The first player to win three games is declared the winner. Depending on time, you may have students play single games to determine a winner.

Major League Soccer Fun

For this activity, you will need to give each participating student a copy of the worksheet titled "Major League Soccer Fun" on page 119. You will also need one die from a pair of dice. This activity will work with one or more students. The beginning of the school year is the best time for this activity.

Have students choose five soccer players from any of the Major League Soccer teams. (The Major League Soccer season usually begins in mid-March.) Encourage students to choose players who usually score goals frequently. Write the players' names in the space provided on the worksheet. Find the number of goals each of the players score in their next games. This process may take a few games because each team will not have a game scheduled on a daily basis. After students find the number of goals for each player, record the total in the space provided below the chart.

Then go to the bottom of the worksheet. Write the total number of goals that their imaginary teams scored in all 10 boxes under the heading "My Score." The "Opponent's Score" will be the number outcome of the roll of one die. For example, for Game 1 the roll of one die is the score of the opponent. Roll the die 10 times to determine the outcome of all 10 games. Write the won/lost record of the team in the space provided at the bottom of the worksheet. Have students circle one of the outcomes at the bottom of the worksheet to see how their teams fared.

Major League Soccer Fun

List five players from Major League Soccer teams below. Write down the number of goals each player scores in his next game.

Player	Team	Goals

Total goals from all five players_____

Use a die from a set of dice. Write the total goals of your five players in the column titled "My Score." Your opponent's score for each game will be the roll of 1 die.

Game	My Score	Opponent's Score
Game 1		
Game 2		
Game 3		
Game 4		
Game 5		
Game 6		
Game 7		
Game 8		
Game 9		
Game 10		

Number of wins _____   Number of losses _____   Number of ties _____

If you had two or fewer losses, you are the MLS Champions!

If you had three or four losses, you made the playoffs but lost in the semifinals.

If you had more than four losses, you need to train harder next year.

Auto Racing Fun

Find an article about an auto racing event in the sports page. Use the race statistics to answer questions on the worksheet below. Use calculators, scratch paper, atlases, or other reference materials as needed.

1. Name the track where this auto racing event was held.

   _____

2. Who won the race? _____

3. What was the average miles per hour of the winner? _____

4. How many miles did those who finished travel? _____

5. If you drove in the race in a car that traveled 65 miles per hour, how long would it take you to finish the race? _____ (Hint: Divide the total race miles by 65 to get time in hours.)

6. How long did it take the winner to finish the race? _____

7. Pretend the winner of the race is driving along the equator. How long would it take him to go around the world if he were traveling at his average race speed? (Hint: The world is about 24,000 miles around the equator.) Write the time in hours and in days. _____

8. If you followed the race winner around the world in your car driving at 60 miles per hour, how long would it take you to circle the world? _____

9. Could the winner of the race make two laps around the world in the same time that you make one? _____

10. How many years would it take the race winner to drive to the sun driving at his average race speed? _____

(L)PGA Tour Fun

Students will need one copy of the workbook page titled "Activity Cards" on page 142 and a copy of the worksheet "(L)PGA Tour Fun" on page 122 for each participant. This activity should be used in conjunction with a PGA tour event or an LPGA tour event. Tour events are held from mid-January through late fall. The opening rounds of golf tournaments are held on Thursdays. Have students start the activity on a Thursday so they can compare their results with the results of actual players by examining the golf leader boards in the Friday sports page. This activity will work equally well with one or more students.

Have students cut the activity cards along the lines. On one card, write the number **3**. On another, write the number **4**. On the next, write **5**. Continue this process until one page of the activity cards is filled with the numbers **3**, **4**, and **5**. Put the numbers in a hat or other container to draw from. Each time a student draws a card, he or she is playing an imaginary hole. The number drawn out of the hat is the score the student will get on the hole. On the worksheet, record the score in the appropriate spot. The students will start on hole number one and continue to draw until they complete 18 holes. Each hole is assigned a par value. The students will either make a par, a bogey, a double bogey, a birdie, or an eagle, depending on the card he or she draws. A **par** is achieved when the number on the card matches the par number on the worksheet. A student makes **bogey** when the number on the card is one number over the par number. A **double bogey** is two numbers over the par value. A student makes **birdie** when the number on the card is one less than the par value. An **eagle** is two less than the par value.

After students complete their 18-hole round, have them add their scores and write the totals in the spaces provided. If students wish to complete all four rounds, allow them to do so. Check the Friday sports page to see how students fared after the first round. On Monday, the final tournament results will be printed in the sports page. Have students add their four-day totals and see where they would place in the tournament. Also, see how much money each student would win by placing him- or herself on the leader board.

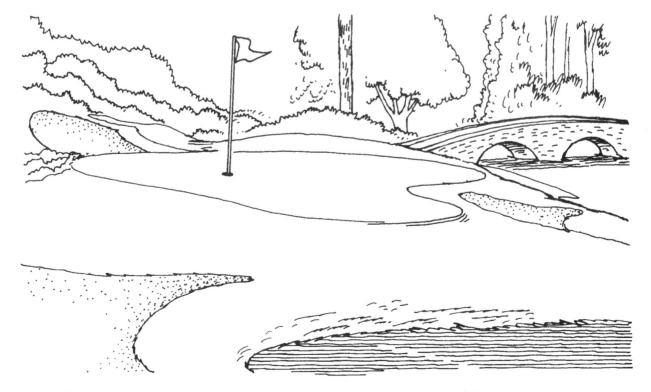

(L)PGA Tour Fun

Worksheet

Play holes 1–18 for each day. Write in all of your scores and total them at the bottom.

Hole Number	Par	Day 1 Scores	Day 2 Scores	Day 3 Scores	Day 4 Scores
1	4				
2	5				
3	3				
4	4				
5	5				
6	4				
7	3				
8	4				
9	4				

9-Hole Score _____ _____ _____ _____

Hole Number	Par	Day 1 Scores	Day 2 Scores	Day 3 Scores	Day 4 Scores
10	4				
11	5				
12	3				
13	4				
14	5				
15	4				
16	3				
17	4				
18	4				

9-Hole Score _____ _____ _____ _____

18-Hole Score _____ _____ _____ _____

Add the four 18-hole scores and write the total here. _____

Look at the Monday sports page. What place did you finish in the tournament? _____

How much money did you earn? _____

Drive for Show, Putt for Dough

In golf there is an old saying: Drive for show, putt for dough. It means that hitting a drive off the tee box a long distance is fun and impressive, but the person who makes the most putts in the fewest tries on the green is the one who usually wins at golf. In this activity, we will examine statistics from two professional golf tours and see if they live up to the old adage, "Drive for show, putt for dough."

Find a sports page with statistics from the two major golf tours in the United States: the PGA tour (Professional Golfers Association) and the LPGA tour (Ladies Professional Golfers Association). The statistics will have many different categories, but you will need to find the ones labeled "Driving Distance, "Putting," and "Money Earnings."

List the top five in each category in the spaces below, then hypothesize about whether or not professional golfers really drive for show and putt for dough.

PGA Tour Leaders

Driving Distance	Putting Leaders	Money Winners
1.	1.	1.
2.	2.	2.
3.	3.	3.
4.	4.	4.
5.	5.	5.

Do professional male golfers appear to earn more money on tour if they drive farther or putt better?

Hypothesize: _____

_____

LPGA Tour Leaders

Driving Distance	Putting Leaders	Money Winners
1.	1.	1.
2.	2.	2.
3.	3.	3.
4.	4.	4.
5.	5.	5.

Do professional female golfers appear to earn more money on tour if they drive farther or putt better?

Hypothesize _____

_____

The Kentucky Derby: Beating the Odds

Each April, the Kentucky Derby is held at Churchill Downs. Oddsmakers place odds on each horse prior to the race. The odds tell what realistic chance each horse has of winning the race. See how the odds below are converted to percentages. Then choose five horses from the sports page the Friday before the Kentucky Derby in April. Change the odds of the horses into percentages.

Odds are written in the form of a ratio. If a horse has the odds 4:1, then the oddsmakers are predicting the horse will win the race one time if the race is run four times (i.e., one out of four). What percent of the time would this particular horse win the race?

❑ First, make a fraction from the ratio: _____.

❑ Then, make the fraction into a decimal: 1 divided by 4 = 0.25.

❑ Now, change the decimal into a percent: 25%. This is accomplished by multiplying 0.25 X 100 or by moving the decimal two places to the right.

This horse has a 25% chance of winning the Derby.

Prior to the race, choose five horses from the sports page. Convert the odds into percentage form in the chart below. Use a calculator, if necessary.

Name of the Horse	Odds	Fraction	Decimal	Percent

Which horse do you think will win the Kentucky Derby? _____

Of the five horses for which you changed odds to percentages, which appears to have the

best chance of winning the Derby? _____

Sports Page Art

Football Player

Find numbers, team logos, and other items from the sports page to use to decorate your sports figure.

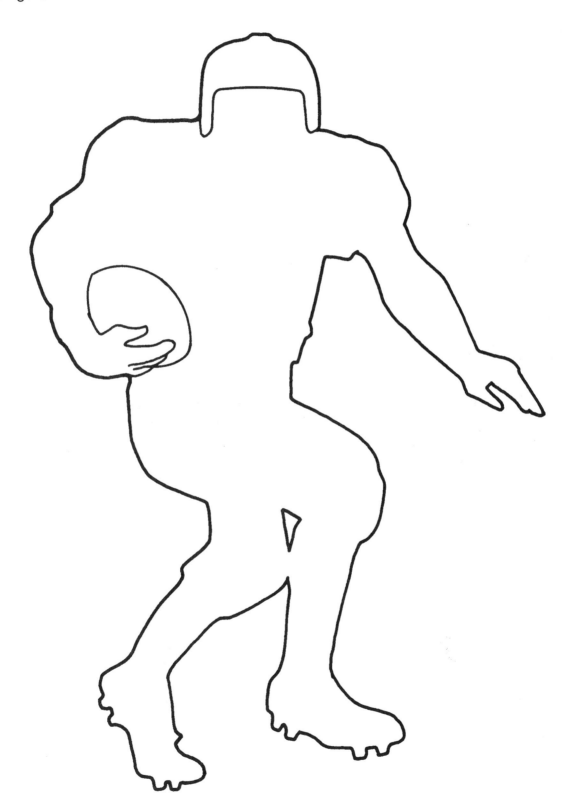

Sports Page Art

Basketball Player

Find numbers, team logos, and other items from the sports page to use to decorate your sports figure.

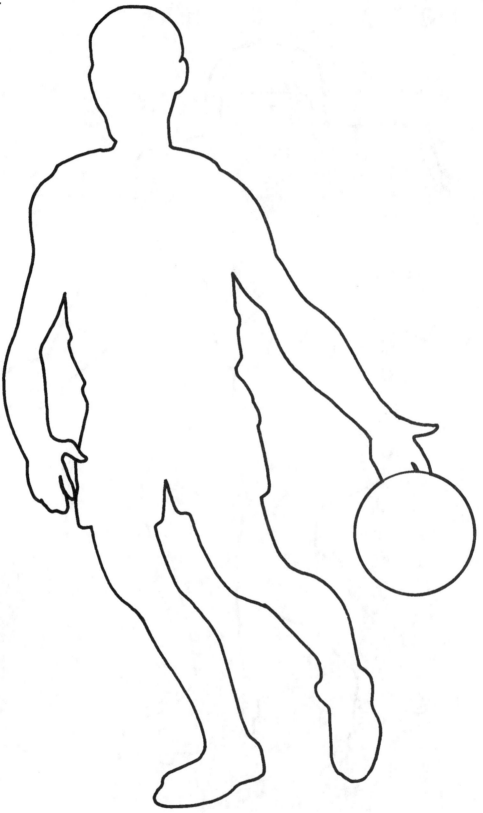

Sports Page Art

Baseball Player

Find numbers, team logos, and other items from the sports page to use to decorate your sports figure.

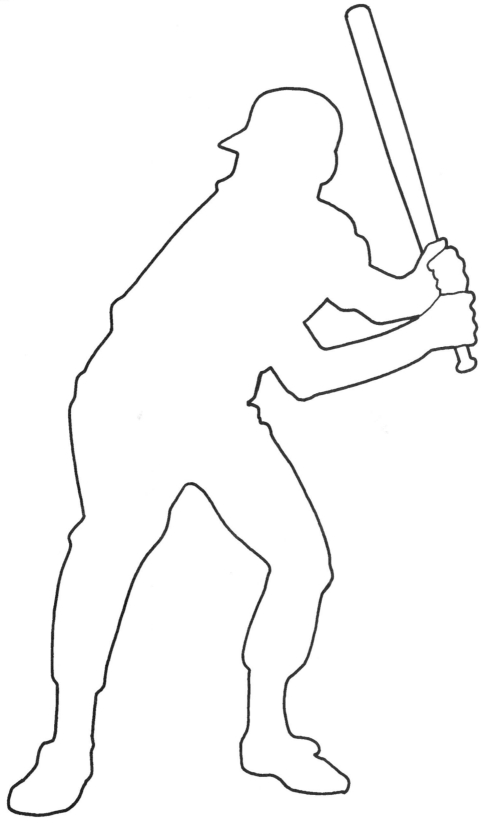

Sports Page Art

Racecar

Find numbers, team logos, and other items from the sports page to use to decorate your racecar. You may wish to cut out your decorated racecar and place it in a racetrack scene.

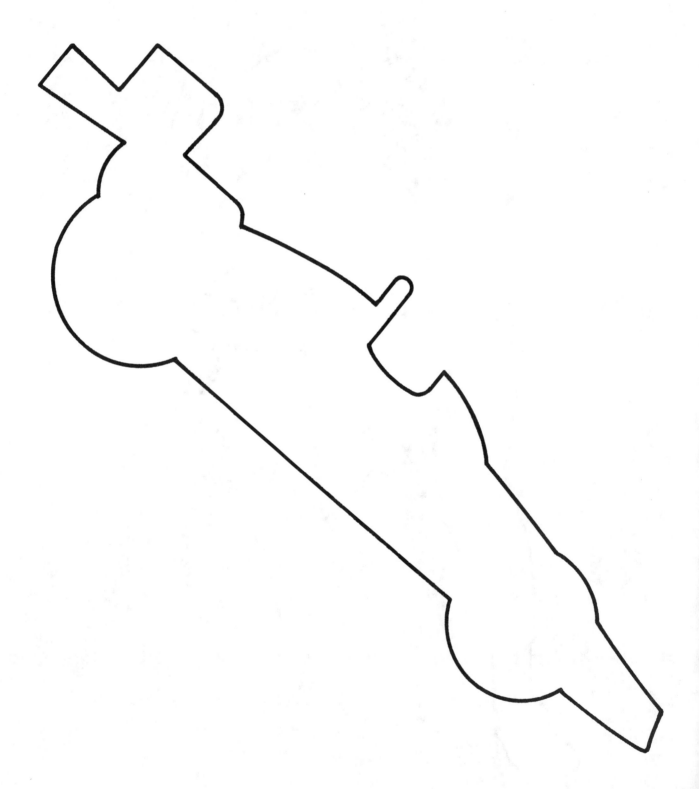

Sports Page Art

Soccer Player

Find numbers, team logos, and other items from the sports page to use to decorate your sports figure.

Sports Page Style Elements

Alliteration

Many sports writers use alliteration, or the repetition of initial sounds, to help them write headlines that grab your attention. Look at the examples below.

Nicked-up Knicks Nudged from playoffs

Hornets Hobbled, But Holding On

Notice how the sounds in the phrases above create an interesting headline. Look through the sports page in your classroom. Find at least three examples of alliteration from the headlines. Cut out your examples and glue them in space below.

Sports Page Style Elements *(cont.)*

Metaphors

Metaphors are prevalent in sports. A metaphor is the comparison of two seemingly unrelated objects or events. Look at the examples below.

The Cardinals exploded in the second half, scoring 35 unanswered points.

After starting slowly, the Cardinals scored a lot of points in the second half. Their offensive output is being compared to a bomb or stick of dynamite that suddenly detonates.

Her rocket of a right arm delivered a perfect throw.

This player has a good throwing arm, and the author compares the speed with which she throws a ball to the velocity of a rocket.

Look at the text and headlines on the sports page to find other examples of metaphors. Cut out your examples and glue them in the space below.

Sports Page Style Elements *(cont.)*

Hyperbole

Hyperbole is the use of exaggeration. Sportswriters use hyperbole often. Look at the examples below to see if you can find the hyperbolic expressions.

As she crossed the finish line, she was running at the speed of sound.

The runner described in this sentence is very fast! But sound travels at 1,200 feet every second. Obviously, no human can approach that speed. The author uses hyperbole to relate to the reader how fast the runner is.

The pole vaulter jumped to the moon before landing on the mat and breaking the world record.

Although the pole vaulter made a great jump, he was not able to jump to the moon. The author uses exaggeration to help the reader form an image of how high the vaulter had to jump to break the record.

Look through the text and headlines of the sports page to find instances where sports columnists used hyperbole. Find as many examples as you can and glue them in the space below.

Sports Page Style Elements *(cont.)*

Similes

A simile is a direct comparison of two objects that are generally not related. The two key words that identify similes are *like* and *as*. Sportswriters use similes in their writing. Look at the examples below.

The ball soared like a bird to left field.

The author compares the flight of a baseball to a bird flying through the air. The word *like* will help you identify this passage as a simile.

Trying to run on the Vandals' defense was as hard as running through a brick wall.

Notice the word *as* in this sentence. Here the Vandals' defense is being compared to a brick wall. Look through the sports page to find some examples of similes. Cut out your examples and glue them in the space provided below.

Sports Page Synonyms

Find words in the sports page that are synonyms for the following words. Cut out and paste your words in the spaces provided.

1. victory _____

2. event _____

3. sprint _____

4. hurt _____

5. throw _____

6. fast _____

7. reception _____

8. score _____

9. middle _____

10. group _____

11. spectator _____

12. division _____

Sports Page Antonyms

Find words in the sports page that are antonyms for each of the following words. Cut out and glue your words in the spaces provided.

1. player _____

2. low _____

3. loss _____

4. catch _____

5. offense _____

6. run _____

7. confident _____

8. weak _____

9. early _____

10. hit _____

11. quiet _____

12. unsuccessful _____

Sports Page Story Hunts

"Sports Page Story Hunts" begin on page 136. Make copies of the worksheets and distribute them to students. You may copy all four stories and pass them out randomly to students or have each student work on the same story. This activity is also well-suited for group learning.

Students will find in the sports page words that fit into the blanks. Encourage students to use words from a headline or byline so that they are more visible to the reader. The results are often humorous. Allow students to share the stories with the class upon completion.

Sports Page Word Hunt

Use the worksheet titled "Sports Page Word Hunt" on page 140 for this activity. Each participating student will need his or her own copy of the worksheet. Students will cut letters from the sports page to fill the grid. Students will hide words to make a word-search puzzle for their peers. Encourage students to use letters from the headlines or bylines so that they are more visible. Have students find teams, players, or sporting events of their choice to place in the grid. It will be easier if students find a place to work and glue these names on the grid before they put on their cover letters. Have students make a word list in the spaces provided on the bottom of the worksheet. You may wish to make a copy of the worksheets when students finish. Then hand out copies of one student's word-find puzzle to the class. Save the other completed worksheets for rainy-day activities.

Sports Page Story Hunt #1

Find in the sports page words that fit in each space. Cut out and glue the words in the spaces.

Yesterday was the big _____. I was more

than nervous. There were so many _____

watching! Even _____ was in the

audience. The score was _____ with less than a

minute left to play. My team had to score. I took the ball on the

_____ yard line. On the first play,

_____ tackled me after a one-yard gain.

But after that, I threw a touchdown pass to _____.

This was a big victory! After the game, our coach told us that the

_____ may be one of the best teams in the

league. The greatest thing happened after the game, though. As I left

the stadium, _____ approached me and asked for

an autograph. I was astounded! If we win next week, we will make the

playoffs. But it won't be easy, because we are playing the

_____ .

Sports Page Story Hunt #2

Find in the sports page words that fit in each space. Cut out and glue the words in the spaces.

_____ has always been my favorite

sport. It is different from other sports. You don't need to rely on other

_____ to participate. You don't even need a

_____ . The weather is important, though. If it's

too _____, you can get in trouble. Not many

_____ come to watch. If you finish first, you

can win a trip to _____. Someday I

want to meet _____. She is the best in this

sport. When she was young, she practiced for _____

hours every day! She injured her _____ last

week so she will not be able to compete in the

_____.

Sports Page Story Hunt #3

Find in the sports page words that fit in each space. Cut out and glue the words in the spaces.

The life of a sports announcer is not always easy. I went to

_____ yesterday to broadcast the _____

game. Then I flew to _____ . I like

covering _____ the best because it is an individual

sport. It seems easy enough, but trying to get the ball over the

_____ is harder than it looks! Another interesting

sport is _____ . The fastest _____

always wins. Sometimes you get to meet famous people such as

_____ . I even went for a ride in a

_____ . Next week I get to watch the

_____ .

Sports Page Story Hunt #4

Find in the sports page words that fit in each space. Cut out and glue the words in the spaces.

_____ came to bat in the bottom of the

_____ inning. _____ was the best

pitcher in the league. The first pitch was high and inside. The next pitch

was called a strike. _____ yelled to swing at the next

pitch no matter what. The crack of the bat signaled a _____.

The runner on _____ base scored easily. The rest of

the _____ went crazy. One fan threw a

_____ on the field. _____ was

named Player of the Game. The next game in

_____ should be easier.

Sports Page Word Hunt

Sports Page Concentration

Use the activity cards on page 142 for this activity. You may wish to fill in the cards yourself or have students find categories in the sports page to list. Make card pairs for this activity. Write team names on one card and city names on the other card. For example, write "Dodgers" on one card and their city, "Los Angeles," on the other card.

Now make the next card set. Write "Minnesota" on one card and their football team, "Vikings," on the other card. Continue in this manner until all the teams in a league are accounted for. (You may also wish to mix leagues on your cards. For example, have 10 football teams and their cities mixed with five baseball teams and their cities.)

When you have a complete set of cards, shuffle them so they are in random order. Then turn them over and number each card on its blank side. Start with one and continue until all the cards are numbered. Next, lay the cards on a table, number side showing. Spread them out so that all the numbered cards are showing. Divide the class or participants into two teams. Ask one of the teams to turn over a card. Imagine card number 11 is turned over and the word "Raiders" appears. The student who turned the card over will look for a match. If he or she is able to turn the word "Oakland" over next, the student would get the total number of points on the cards for the matching set. For example, if the Raiders is card number 11 and Oakland is card number 6, the team would receive 17 total points. If a matching set is found, have that team take those cards off the table. If the student is unable to match a pair, turn the cards facedown again and give the other team a chance to match a pair.

As the game goes on, students will start to remember where some of the cards are from their failed attempts. You may wish to have a member from each team keep score on the board. The team with the most points after all the cards have been matched wins the game.

After you make a set of cards, you may wish to laminate them and save them for future use. Use local teams. Use different combinations of players, teams, and sports. Make a set of cards listing players on their teams, using the headlines from the sports page. Cut out a player's name from the headlines and glue it on a card. Then cut out his or her sport and glue on another card. Shuffle the cards and number as described above. Allow students to make card sets in their spare time for extra credit. Hold weekly Sports Page Concentration competitions. Set up a concentration center where students can go when they finish an assignment.

Sports Page Twenty Questions

Find the worksheet labeled "Activity Cards" on page 142 of the workbook. Make a copy, and give each student in your class one card. Students will also need a sports page and a pencil.

Allow students to look through the sports page to find words to write on their cards. Each word may be a sport, a player, an event such as the Rose Bowl, or any item of choice. After all the members of the class have finished, ask for a volunteer to come to the front of the class. His or her classmates will get to ask the student 20 questions to try to figure out the word. Remember that a simple "yes" or "no" must answer each question. The game is over when the class figures out the word or when 20 questions have been asked. Allow another volunteer to follow.

Activity Cards

The Draft

1.	2.	3.
4.	5.	6.
7.	8.	9.
10.	11.	12.
13.	14.	15.
16.	17.	18.
19.	20.	21.
22.	23.	24.
25.	26.	27.
28.	29.	30.

Scavenger Hunt Answer Sheet

1.	2.
3.	4.
5.	6.
7.	8.
9.	10.